A **HOLIDAY** MAGAZINE

TRAVEL GUIDE

ROME

The *Holiday* Guide to

ROME

Prepared with the cooperation of the editors of HOLIDAY magazine.

RANDOM HOUSE
 NEW YORK

Copyright © 1960, 1962, 1964, 1966, 1968, 1971, 1973, 1976
by the Curtis Publishing Company
All rights reserved under International and Pan-American
Copyright Conventions. Published in the United States by
Random House, Inc., New York, and simultaneously in
Canada by Random House of Canada Limited, Toronto.

Library of Congress Cataloging in Publication Data
Main entry under title:

The Holiday guide to Rome.

(The Holiday magazine travel guide series ; 6)
Previous editions published under title: Rome.
Includes index.
1. Rome (City)—Description—Guide-books. I. Holiday.
II. Series.
DG804.R6827   1976   914.5′04′92   75–32501
ISBN 0–394–73201–4

Manufactured in the United States of America
2 4 6 8 9 7 5 3
Revised Edition

CONTENTS

CHAPTER 1

ROME: THE PRESENT

To understand Rome in its true richness and variety, you will have to go and see for yourself. In doing so, more than likely you will share the feelings of Fenimore Cooper, one of the first American visitors to Rome. He said he was "stupefied as a countryman who first visits town, perplexed with the whirl of sensations and the multiplicity of the objects."

Afterward, after the first or the hundredth visit, you will be asked what you think of the city. And the chances are that faced with the enormous question of Rome, you too will have to shrug—in the eloquent Italian language of gestures—and begin with the same old cliché, "There's no place like it." Like most clichés, there is a good deal of truth in it. Rome *is* different from any other city, proud and conscious of its difference. And *place* is the key to knowing and loving the city.

In the old days (about the time that Henry James first came to Rome and ran in the streets for the joy of being there and wrote in his journal, "At last for the first time I live!"), you came to Rome by means of a bouncy uncomfortable coach, moving slowly over bad roads, sweating and fuming. At a certain point, a rise in the ground, the coachman pulled up his horses, slacked off the reins, and pointed dead ahead with the butt of his whip. "*Ecco Roma*," he said. And he waited long enough for his passengers to savor the moment and to distinguish with the sudden joyous tug of fulfillment the great impossible and beautiful dome of St. Peter's hovering above the edge of the horizon as light and airy as a balloon on a string.

Nowadays the roads are good and swift, the trains are swifter, and you may arrive from almost anywhere in a jet-powered airliner. But,

Piazza Venezia, heart of ancient and modern Rome

however you happen to get there, there is still that breath-taking first moment, like love at first sight, when Rome appears. Rome has no real suburbia in our sense of the word, and you come on the city abruptly. It seems to grow out of the ground, to be part and parcel of the rich and fertile earth all around it. Color has a lot to do with this initial impression. Colors of Italian earth and stone predominate in Rome. Houses and buildings, villas, palaces, churches, and monuments are in many subtle shades of tan and brown and yellow and gray. Against all of it the white shining marble of the Victor Emmanuel Monument glows like a lighted birthday cake. (You can't miss this monument from any view of the city, and whether you think of it as a thing of beauty, like some, or a pure monstrosity, like many others, you learn to use it as a kind of North Star to guide your navigations around the city.) New York is shine, glitter, and soaring aspiration. London is the grand gray dowager, formidable, superbly mannered, and a bit old-fashioned. Paris is the city of autumnal gray, the uniform gray of enormous nostalgia. But Rome is a city of the earth, eroded by time, the weather, and the seasons, but always a living thing. In bright sunlight on a fine day Rome seems to sway and dance like a tree in the breeze.

The four seasons are kind to Rome. Fall is subdued and gradual, winter is mild and wet—a little like winter in Charleston, South Carolina. Spring explodes in an overwhelming display of lushness. It is all blooming, with flowers growing brightly everywhere and banked high in the street-corner flower stalls like fugues of color. Summer is warm (sometimes hot) and dry but manages somehow to preserve most of the pleasant surprises of spring. The truth is, though no Roman will admit it, Rome was built for the hot season. High-ceilinged, stone rooms are cool and shadowy and seem eminently suited to the weather. In summer too you learn to appreciate the real reason for the multitude of fountains; for Rome is fountains, large and small, spraying high, falling, or merely trickling everywhere you turn. The sound of water falling and the sight of ghostly jets and sprays is as kind and cooling as air conditioning on a summer's day.

You are never very far from the weather and the effect of the seasons in Rome. Green blends everywhere with the earth colors of the buildings. There are great parks and acres of ruins, like the Palatine Hill, where grass and ivy scrawl a silent epitaph on old glories. There are dozens of palaces—many of them now apartment houses and office buildings—where the main gate opens into a courtyard of green. You stumble on these open gates as you pass by on the narrow busy sidewalks, and if you are, like the Romans themselves, patient, persistent, and polite, there are few porters who will deny you the privilege of stepping inside for just a moment to see and share the beauty. Seen from a hill, one of the celebrated seven or, even better, from the Janiculum across the Tiber, Rome seems to be at least half green. It is a city of many trees, and the great trees of the city, the cypress, palm, and pine, are evergreen. It is very much an outdoor city, wedded to its earth and its weather. People hang bird cages outdoors so that the birds can share the seasons and add their songs to the noise of the streets.

Of course no city is just an arrangement of buildings, streets, and parks. Except, maybe, a ghost town. Rome may be full of ghosts and haunted by the memories of a long, full, and complex history, but it is no ghost town. Life throbs in all the streets, and Rome is its people. Nothing, certainly no arrangement of words on a page, can really prepare the visitor for the experience of a Roman street. Buses and trams compete with the swift darting little cars for an inch of the limited space. There are carriages and horse carts and bicycles and motorscooters. And motorcycles! Hondas and Harley Davidsons weave and dodge like scatbacks through the rush. They buzz along like deranged bumblebees, narrowly averting a dozen imminent collisions, and roar onward, often with a beautiful Roman girl, skirt billowing, riding a graceful, poised sidesaddle behind the driver. And then there are the pedestrians, brave and untroubled ones who seem never to have accepted the fact that the internal-combustion engine is here to stay. They don't walk, they *stroll* in the streets, adding immeasurably to the chaos.

This surge of traffic, like a stampede, like a riptide, occurs not twice but four times a day because of the leisurely siesta after lunch. At first sight it seems almost too formidable to be dared. The rules of the road are few. Stop signs and street lights are rare—and often completely unheeded. At many big corners it is every driver for himself. As a driver you have no choice but to relax and enjoy it. The curious thing is that in a very short time American visitors to Rome find themselves driving in the best Roman style. And it *works*. Why, nobody is quite sure. Perhaps it is because of the wonderful traffic police with their London bobby hats and their long, immaculate white gloves. With the courage and bravado of lion tamers and the grace of ballet dancers they stand in the midst of it all and keep it rolling. (They never seem to lose their tempers, good manners, or forget the quick smile and snappy salute with which they greet you when you have a problem or a question to ask. They are ready to give directions and all carry maps of the city. If you *do* happen to get into trouble of one kind or another, the Roman traffic policeman is apt to discuss it with you at some length and from every conceivable point of view; then just when you're resigned to the fact of a traffic ticket, he's apt to shrug and wave you on your way.) Maybe the reason that the Roman traffic snarl unwinds four times a day successfully is that the traffic problem, like everything else to the Romans, is an old, old problem. Julius Caesar had to cope with it. And maybe the real reason that order comes out of confusion is that the people of Rome are astonishingly polite and considerate. A Roman driver will maintain *bella figura* (the Roman equivalent of the Oriental idea of "face")

View of St. Peter's from the Palatine Hill

only up to a certain point. He will not die for it or for the right of way. He isn't trying to prove anything. He loves his car and his life too much. Life is too good to him to be gambled away.

If you decide to avoid coping with traffic yourself and leave the driving to a bus driver—what living monuments of patience those bus drivers are—you have to face the problem of another kind of crowd. At times the buses and trams bulge at the seams with mankind packed and stuffed into every available inch. But, once again, the Romans display an amazing natural politeness even at close quarters. You board a bus or tram from the rear, pay your fare to a seated conductor, and then begin the struggle to move forward and be in a position to get off. If you aren't willing to play this Roman game, you may ride far beyond your destination. You have to move steadily forward against a phalanx of flesh and bones. There's no reason to be shy, though. You simply suppress your natural reticence, and you push and shove your way, always nodding and smiling, to the exit door. Everyone else is doing the same thing at the same time. Somehow it works too. In fact, the public transportation in Rome is remarkably efficient.

In close crowds anywhere, though, you really ought to be careful of your wallet or your purse. Rome has very few crimes of violence compared to other cities of its size, but the picking of a stranger's pocket is a fine art. Women should be especially wary of purse snatchers who work in pairs on motorcycles. One does the snatching while the other keeps the motor roaring for the get-away.

As strange as it may seem, the Romans respect any attempt to speak their language. Unlike the French or the Germans, for example, the Romans won't correct you or simply fail to understand your faulty grammar and wretched accent. They are pleased that you will try to speak their language. They try their best to understand you, and, if you're not careful, you may find that they try to speak a kind of pidgin Italian like yours, so that *you* can understand them. This is not because the Romans have no pride in their language; it may be because the Romans love to talk so much that they don't intend a little matter like a difference in languages to deprive them of the pleasures of conversation and gossip.

Part of the natural warmth and easygoing charm of the Romans is due to the rhythm of their daily lives. In the north of Italy heavy industry has set its own demanding schedule. In the south stark poverty has fixed another. But in Rome the schedule of the day is designed for all to enjoy the pleasures of living. Romans like to eat and eat well, and, rich and poor alike, they close up shop, lay down shovel and hoe at lunch time. Luncheon is no midday snack; it is a big meal, leisurely and festive, and it is always followed by a long siesta. Many people actually put on pajamas and go to bed during these hours. Rome comes very close to being a ghost town between one o'clock and four in the afternoon. This is sometimes infuriating to visitors with limited time and so much to do and see. It shouldn't be. For at four o'clock the city springs to life again. Everything opens wide and stays open until eight-thirty or nine. After a morning of sightseeing, you come to welcome the relaxed luncheon, the sudden hush of the city, and the chance to rest and collect yourself. You can, if you wish, wander along almost empty streets; you can sleep. You even have time to read a book. The Romans are notorious nonreaders. But there are many bookshops in Rome which carry a representative selection of the best new books in foreign languages including English. You find that the siesta is a most civilized custom.

Dinner comes late. It too is a large and pleasantly dawdling affair. And afterward there are illuminated fountains and vistas to see— most Romans take a walk in the evening, dressed in their finest, to see these things—and good movies, the theater, concerts, and opera. But Rome is not, like Paris, a city of prolonged night life. Things quiet down early. By midnight scarcely anything is moving. This can be a glorious time for a visitor. With most of Rome in bed it is easy to go quickly to a favorite *piazza,* fountain, or view and to enjoy it in relative solitude. The party is over, but the eternal city is still very much there and can be enjoyed intimately.

One of the buildings of the vast E.U.R.

There are many ways to see Rome, almost as many as there are things to be seen; that is, the possibilities are almost infinite. Still, almost everyone, from the lifetime expatriate resident to the visitor on a three-day tour, has his favorites, the special places that come to mean a great deal just by being there. Midnight or early morning are fine times to enjoy them.

The place, the people, the rhythm of a way of life, are attractive and unique. But why, after all, are you really there, and what were you expecting? You have come to a city, a great and celebrated city, which has never died. You have come as a kind of pilgrim, like countless thousands before you, to the beating heart of the Western world. One of the reasons that Rome seems to be an enchanted place is that so many expectations are fulfilled, so many vague dreams realized. It is almost as if you had been there before. You have come to meet your own history, and it is there, everywhere, all around you. Wherever you go there are famous ruins from the days when Rome was no more than a rude collection of tribal huts and other relics through the ages down to our own time when Rome was briefly the center of a bogus balcony empire. Layer upon layer of human history is visible and tangible, written into the pattern of the city like the strata of ancient mountains or the rings of a venerable tree. You might imagine that it would be a little depressing to visit such a museum of ruined time. It would be so, if Rome *were* a museum, and it was so for many a 19th-century traveler who reveled in the picturesque aspects of de-

Part of the ancient Servian Wall

A corner of fashionable Via Vittorio Veneto

cline and decay. It is not a museum for the modern visitor. A magnificent modern city thrives among ruins and monuments. They complement each other beautifully and hospitably. Perhaps this is no better illustrated than in the new railroad station, the *Stazione Termini*, a soaring structure of contemporary beauty composed of steel and concrete and glass with a graceful cantilevered roof. Nearby, in fact joining the building, is a piece of the Servian Wall, the oldest of the Roman walls still standing. Parts of that wall are used functionally in the interior of the station. The oldest and newest go together hand in hand, amiable and equal.

It is in this sense that Rome is an inspiring city. It is not yet one with Nineveh and Tyre. It does not, like Athens for example, sit in the mocking shadow of past glories. The buildings old and new, the ruins, and the broken ground where new apartment houses and buildings will be going up all seem to combine to say the same thing —that there is a meaning in human history, that history has direction and purpose, though it may never be what we suspect or wish. Rome says eloquently that all our buildings will one day be ruins too, but others will rise in the same place. And some of ours will remain to be viewed and cherished by tourists in a world we cannot even imagine. Meanwhile, Rome and the Romans say in one voice, life goes on. The city and its people welcome you to it. As a guest you will never be able to change it. (Even the Roman faults are ancient and here to stay.) It *is* likely that you will be changed by being in Rome, imperceptibly perhaps, knocked off by a couple of degrees from whatever balance of certainties you arrived with. Changed or unchanged, you are certain to be gratified. For once you pay your money you get not only your choice and your money's worth, but more than money can buy.

You may come once or a hundred times to the city. You may see Rome in one brief season or through all four, but whatever you do, you are bound to find someone else who wants to go there and will ask you, "What is Rome really like?" You pause, consider a moment, shrug and begin, "There is no place like it. . . ."

CHAPTER 2

ROME: THE PAST

The legendary founding of Rome by Romulus and Remus is commemorated in statues and emblems all over the city. The wolf which suckled them is even more vividly commemorated. A live she-wolf is kept in a cage near the top of the splendid Renaissance stairway leading to the Capitol as a memento. She seems well fed, comfortable, and calm.

The authentic beginnings of Rome, clusters of tribal huts on top of the seven hills, have appeared among the fairly recent excavations on the Palatine Hill. There you can see a natural stone foundation, on which once rested the poles or crude beams of a primitive hut. And all around this simple spot sprawl the layers of ruined brick from the later great days of imperial Rome.

This was an ideal location for a group of tribesmen who wanted to band together and make a town. The seven hills were seven natural forts, and the Janiculum Hill, on the other side of the Tiber River, was like a protective wall. Then there was the river itself, which was both a good line of defense and also navigable. The Tiber thus gave Rome access to the sea. But the sea was far enough away to protect the town from sea raiders, and give it the peace to thrive.

Nobody knows much about the long period in which tribal Rome gradually became a kingdom and then a republic. Names and legends have been handed down, but no authentic history until about the 5th century B.C. By the time there is anything in the way of historical records Rome was already a republic. Of the time before that we have a few stories and the names of some kings, some mythical, some real. The last of these kings appears to have been from the family line of some Etruscans called Tarquin.

Columns of the Temple of Apollo

The Etruscans are today a mysterious and fascinating people. A current theory and some recent evidence suggests that they migrated to Italy from Sardis in Asia Minor. They had cities and a developed civilization when Rome was still a few huts. It was a civilization very different from the Roman one which eventually replaced it. Artistic, sensual, religious, the Etruscans seemed to lack the interest or ambition to match Roman practicality. The lost civilization of the Etruscans has lately enjoyed a renaissance of interest and admiration. Perhaps the chief reason for this is the beauty of their art which has endured undisturbed in tombs for centuries. It is a surprisingly modern art, and many modern painters and sculptors have found inspiration in their wall paintings, bronzes, and ceramics. Rome has wonderful collections of these Etruscan survivals in the *Capitoline Museum,* in the *Villa Albani*, and especially in the *Villa Giulia*, a splendid museum devoted exclusively to Etruscan studies. To the ancient Romans these objects were contemptible. To the modern eye they are aesthetically beautiful. And even those who are unmoved by art are delighted and amused by many of the pots and bronzes which are shamelessly bawdy.

The original town of Rome was formed on the Palatine Hill. Remains of early walls have been excavated there. Below the hill was the marshy stretch of ground which was one day to become the Forum, and directly across the way is the Capitoline Hill. Under the Tarquin kings the seven hills of Rome were bound together under one rule, and the Romans gave the world a hint of their future intentions by incorporating other people's land up and down the river. The future engineering prowess of the Romans was prefigured in early temples and in the great sewer, the *Cloaca Maxima,* which still drains into the Tiber in the heart of the city. And it was during the time of the Tarquin kings that the Servian Wall was built around the entire city as it then stood.

In due time the Tarquin dynasty was expelled and replaced by an aristocratic republic. It managed to last for about 500 years. During this long Republican period Rome became a modest little empire, secured its position in Italy—though not before being captured and thoroughly sacked for the first time by the Gauls around 390 B.C.— and, more important to the modern visitor, the Forum became the center of Roman life and activity.

Many are inevitably disappointed with the first view of the Forum. It seems so *small,* and, except for the great arch and some tall lonely columns, so little is left standing. It is remarkable that there is anything left to stand up or be dug up by archeologists, since it was used for centuries as a quarry. The marble of half the palaces and churches in Rome comes from there. For the travelers of a hundred years ago, before any real excavation got under way, it must have been even more disappointing, though our grandparents did love the picturesque and were always ready for ruins. By the 19th century the Forum had returned to its original condition—it was a good-sized cow pasture.

But during the great days of Rome, the Forum was the center of the civilized world. It has to be peopled by the mind's eye to be believed. And we have to shed the school-acquired notion of a white marble place, like a huge museum, patrolled by languid tiptoing figures clad in togas. The Forum began as a market, remained a market place for many years, and even at its most distinguished, when the pedlars had been banished to other parts of the city, it was a business district. The atmosphere of a large open-air market can be seen in Rome today, in the big market in *Trastevere* or the "flea market" near the *Porta Portese*. They have all the bustle, color, and activity of a carnival, and since the buyers and sellers are Romans they also have the noise, the sound of hundreds of voices talking and bargaining all at once. In the old Forum, in the middle of all this market confusion, the toga-style business was moving too, same place, same time. Among other things the Forum was the judicial center. Open-air courts held trials of all kinds. Political oratory, with all the famous Latin pyrotechnics, rang across the crowd. Banking and big business were in full swing, and from time to time games and exhibitions were presented there. It was Wall Street, Tammany Hall, Broadway, Madison Square Garden, and Union Square, all rolled into one.

If you wish to put faces on the imaginary people of the Forum, you have only to visit the *Capitoline Museum* of sculpture, not far away, where there are rooms full of portrait busts dating from republican and imperial Rome. They are all there, fat ones and thin ones, shrewd and stupid, the bad guys and the good. In no time you can conjure up a world.

Now the Forum is silent. The traffic of the city flows all around it without actually encroaching on its small green space dotted with marble fragments. A fine time to see it and to think of the early days of Rome, to indulge in a little pure nostalgia, is by night when it is skillfully and subtly illuminated. And a fine place to see it from is the backside of the Capitoline Hill. There is a vantage point halfway down where horse carriages and a few late cars pull up to view the muted ghost of Roman glory.

Via Dei Fori Imperiali, looking toward the Colosseum

Tombs along Via Appia Antica; One of the Dioscuri

During the days of the republic, Rome weathered storms and wars and began to be a real empire. Riches poured in, and with power and riches came corruption, internal strife, and commercial slavery. This slavery, slavery on a very large scale, is a most important factor in understanding the background of Rome. There is hardly a relic of the ancient times that is not the result of an inexhaustible labor supply made up of sweating, unpaid slaves. Lacking the enormous machinery of modern technology, they made do with many hands. In those confused and expanding times it was no wonder that Rome got its first look at rule by popular dictator. The most popular and powerful of these, and the only avowed dictator, was Julius Caesar. His ghost still haunts the city. You can see the very stones Mark Anthony stood on when he delivered the funeral oration in the Forum. (Contrary to popular notion, Caesar wasn't killed in the Forum. The Senate was meeting elsewhere at the time, in the *Theater of Pompey*.)

After the dictator's fall and the period of strife that followed, the reign of the first emperor, Augustus, introduced the high-flying days of imperial Rome. It was a great period of art and architecture and public works. Most of the remaining Roman ruins, the roads, tombs, arches, columns, theaters, the Coliseum, and the Pantheon—which, by the way, is the one fully preserved Roman structure—date from the long imperial period. It wasn't particularly tranquil. After the Augustan Age came the Julian and Claudian emperors, including such figures as Caligula and Nero. There were good emperors as well. One favorite of moderns is Hadrian, who collected discriminatingly from the art of the known world, and adorned Rome with the Pantheon and his tomb, now known as the Castel Sant'Angelo; and not far from the city are the ruins of his incredible villa, now a lovely picnic spot.

For some of the beauty and decorum of the good life in imperial Rome the visitor should see the *Museo Nazionale Romano,* across from the *Termini Station*, among the ruins of the *Baths of Diocletian*. There are famous and beautiful statues from antiquity, elegantly displayed, mosaics shown as they ought to be with a thin film of clear water above the bright multicolored stones, wall paintings, and many artifacts. They make it easier to imagine how the people who ran that show really lived. The triumphal arches, such as those of Titus, Constantine, Septimius Servus, the obelisks in the streets and squares of Rome, give an adequate impression of the public face of the imperial period. The Palatine Hill has the ruins of the imperial palaces, but it is hard to conjure up from a few brick foundations the Palace of Domitian. The *Museo Nazionale Romano* may come very close to suggesting to the visitor the kind of life the great men knew in private, behind the imperial façade.

There was something else going on in imperial Rome, something which must have seemed to those in power to be a temporary and vexing minor internal problem. The subversive Christians were there. The plain cross standing in the center of the Coliseum and the savage early frescoes of martyrdoms on the walls of *St. Stefano Rotundo* are permanent testimony to the unbelievable persecutions they suffered, endured, and triumphed over. For the visitor who would like to get a feeling of what it was like to be one of these subversives in imperial Rome, there are the famous catacombs out along the *Via Appia Antica*. A smaller and perhaps more unified experience lies beneath the medieval *Church of San Clemente*. You pay a small entrance fee to the Irish monks who maintain the church, and then descend two levels. There in a darkness fitfully lighted by occasional naked bulbs, a darkness troubled by the rushing sound of water flowing underneath the foundations, you can stand in one of the oldest preserved Christian meeting places in the world. Adjoining the Christian church is a small Mithraic temple. Both cults were outlawed and clandestine in the beginning. It is somehow suitably ironic that it fell the duty of the Christians, once they were in power and the official religion, to stamp out the cult of Mithra.

Imperial Rome lasted a long time and left much behind, much that survived even attempts by the early Popes to wipe out its memory. The Renaissance recovered Western Man's admiration for the Classical era. Perhaps the whole of imperial Rome is summed up in the square on top of the Capitoline Hill by the great bronze statue of Marcus Aurelius which stands there. Michelangelo placed it in the center of this *piazza* which he designed. It is an equestrian statue and the only surviving equestrian of ancient Rome. The emperor, stern and larger than life, one hand raised in salute or benediction, is all that an emperor should be. Michelangelo himself said all that can be said of the horse in one word. The story is that when he first viewed the statue, he spoke to the horse. "Walk!" he commanded.

The Empire slowly declined. The boundaries shrank. Barbarian enemies seized and sacked the city a number of times. By 476 A.D. it was clearly all over. Barbarians ruled, the population had dwindled considerably. (At its height the population of ancient Rome had been somewhere between one and two million.) Great buildings, like the fortunes of the place, fell into disrepair and decay.

But Rome was now a Christian city, the center of Christendom. Even before the fall of Rome, the city had become increasingly ecclesiastical. And the rebirth of the new city was to be effected by the Church. Pope Leo I wrote, "St. Peter and St. Paul are the Romulus and Remus of the new Rome, as much superior to the old as truth is to error." Goths and Lombards came and conquered, but the Church continued to grow and gain in power. It is true that the stones of many famous pagan buildings were used to build new structures for the Church, but it is also true, as Pope Leo I implied, that some of the strength of the Church derived from its ability to *incorporate* the old into the new. This can be seen today all over Rome in churches which use the columns of earlier pagan buildings for supports. And one of the finest and best preserved of the Roman temples, the *Temple of Virile Fortune,* was converted intact into a Christian church. Just like the modern Romans, the Christianized Romans thought of the past as something to be used as much as honored.

During the long medieval period, Rome experienced fantastic ups and downs. There were memorable moments like the coronation of Charlemagne as Holy Roman Emperor, the king kneeling to receive his crown from the Pope on Christmas Day 800. There were dark times with the papacy and its power in decadence, Rome weak and underpopulated, alien Saracens prowling the coasts and once even sacking the basilicas of St. Peter's and St. Paul's. Kings and powerful nobles and corrupt politicians, within and without the Church, battled for power. A moment of complete degradation came when Pope Boniface VIII, sitting on his throne in full pontifical robes, was literally dragged down and narrowly escaped being stabbed on the spot. More than one Pope had to flee along the secret walk from the Vatican gardens to the security of the Castel Sant'Angelo. When the Renaissance reached Rome, it was to find the people ready for something new; during the Middle Ages they had endured everything.

Medieval Rome is very much present in the tortuous, picturesque side streets of the *Trastevere* section, and as well in the back streets on the other side of the Tiber. These are dark, narrow, and beautifully preserved medieval streets which parallel some of the main arteries of the city. One shouldn't miss taking a walk along a street like the *Via Monserrato.* The medieval period is also represented in the stern·and gloomy Castel Sant'Angelo and in Romanesque churches like *San Clemente* and *Santa Maria in Cosmedin,* the latter dominated by its tall bell tower. The churches themselves are like fortresses against the host of enemies outside, thick-walled, with few windows, true sanctuaries in a chaotic world. But the quiet interior side of medieval Christian life is perhaps best illustrated by the cloister of the church of *Quattro Coronati* ("Four Crowned Saints"). You enter the church through strong defensible walls, pass through the church itself, open a heavy old door, and you are in a medieval cloister. A small fountain plays discreetly in the center, roses are growing in pro-

Sant' Angelo Bridge and Castel Sant' Angelo

fusion, and there is a hush like the silence at the heart of the deep woods. (Actually you are in the center of the modern city.) It is a timeless place of prayer and meditation and a home for an order of cloistered nuns who have taken vows of silence. When you see the Castel Sant'Angelo, looming like a huge doubled fist over the Tiber, you can picture the swarm of troubles that made such a fort a necessity. You view the cloister of *Quattro Coronati,* simple and beautiful and somehow outside of history, and you are able to sense the strength of the life that triumphed over dark times. You remember that Rome is a city of many saints.

Florence is, of course, the true jewel of the Renaissance. It presents for inspection a unified and composite picture of that age of great changes and marvels. The Renaissance lives on in Rome too, but differently. The great examples of Renaissance architecture, the palaces, villas, churches, and amazing squares—explosions of light and air and space entered by dark streets—must rub shoulders with past and present. The Renaissance was in Rome, as elsewhere in Italy, a great age, a peak in history, and it was this age that gave to the city as a whole its character and general appearance. Paradoxically, it wasn't politically or socially a more tranquil time than the Middle Ages had been. If anything, it was a period of greater turmoil. It is said to have been ushered in grimly by the Black Death of 1378 which took seven out of ten Roman lives. Noble families continued to fight each other, tooth and nail, like dogs over a bone. Dictators and tyrants rose and fell. The practical philosophy of Machiavelli prevailed.

Fontana Del Moro, one of three in Piazza Navona

But this same period was also one of the greatest periods of art and learning the Western world has ever known. There are times in human history when it seems that art alone expresses the true ideals and aspirations of a people and a society. The Renaissance is one of these periods. The names of most of the great politicians, tyrants, and re-formers alike, are dust. The works of the artists live on. The hopes, ideals, and highest desires of Western man are written ineffaceably into the stones of Rome.

The fine arts bloomed as never before. The palace galleries and public museums of Rome today glitter like open jewel boxes with a representative selection of the work of most of the important Renaissance painters, from the fumbling beginnings through the High Renaissance with its great roster of names like Leonardo, Michelangelo, Titian, Raphael, and innumerable others, on through Correggio and up to the 16th century, which the Italians call the *Cinquecento.* In architecture the signature and influence of the great men is to be seen everywhere. St. Peter's and the Vatican are symbols of the best of the Renaissance, at once highly individual and collaborative. Bramante shares with Michelangelo and Raphael (and later Bernini) an equal part in making St. Peter's what it is today. Yet, true to the Renaissance ideal of diversity, Bramante also built the tiny domed building, called the *Tempietto,* in the cloister of the little *Church of San Pietro in Montorio,* not far from St. Peter's. The whole church is of interest to American visitors, since it was built by Ferdinand and Isabella of Spain, who accidentally financed the discovery of our continent. It is also of considerable architectural interest: the dome of the *Tempietto* was the model for our Capitol in Washington. For a sense of the Renaissance ideals of beauty, harmony, and proportion, one has only to stand and look at the *piazza* Michelangelo designed for the Capitol in Rome or at the façade of St. Peter's—monumental, yet perfectly proportioned. For a view of the richness of the interior life, luxurious and stately, the palaces offer much, for example, the public gallery of the *Palazzo Doria.*

For the *source* of many of the Renaissance artistic ideals, the statues and artifacts of classical antiquity in the Vatican museum tell us a great deal; for it was during this same period that intelligent antiquarian interest and some heavy digging brought to light many of our links with ancient Rome and Greece.

About a generation ago the prevailing critical view was that art fell into decadence after the Renaissance. The artists of the *Cinquecento* and their followers had different ideals and interests and were generally thought to be inferior to their predecessors. Great critics, such as Bernard Berenson, who had focused the modern world's attention on the unique beauties of the Renaissance, were in part responsible for the widespread notion that the artists who followed somehow had lost touch with the great tradition. They were more elaborate, fantastic, full of surprises, and much concerned with exuberant virtuosity. Our own art of the 1930's helped to solidify this view. We accepted as gospel the idea that material should be expressed directly in a work of art. That is to say, marble ought to look like marble and not, as Bernini made it, like flesh real enough to make the viewer dare a tentative touch. The folly of such an absolute judgment has been pretty well exposed now, and it is once again all right to admire the joyful extravagances of Baroque art with which Rome abounds. (Everybody did all along, it turns out, but secretly.)

At the peak of the Baroque period Bernini stands as the leading sculptor and designer and Caravaggio is the painter. Both are very well represented throughout Rome, and the work of both artists is found in plentitude together in the *Villa Borghese*. A tour of the gallery is like a tour through the Baroque.

The Reformation, coming at the end of the Renaissance, resulted in the fragmentation of Christendom and inevitably some decline in the importance of Rome as its center. Never really united since imperial days, Italy was a welter of weak, separate kingdoms. By the 18th century Italy, with Rome as its focus, was becoming one of the things that it is today, a second home for tourists and visitors from the world over.

The French Revolution at the end of the 18th century produced the first leader in a modern sense—Napoleon. Naturally Rome did not escape his influence. By 1805 he was wearing the Iron Crown of the Kingdom of Italy. The following year he put an end to the moribund Holy Roman Empire once and for all. His effect on Rome itself was of brief duration, but permanent. He had a certain appeal to the people who had known the Caesars and were later to know Mussolini. Napoleon packed off huge quantities of Roman art to Paris. (You can see many of these things today at the Louvre.) His mother lived out her life in the Bonaparte Palace on the Corso. His sister Pauline married a Borghese prince and was immortalized in marble by Canova. You can see her, half-nude, pensive, a little amused, in the Villa Borghese. The Prince Borghese, who had never been a jealous man. kept the statue locked up and he had the only key.

After the French Revolution and after the impact of Napoleon, the whole of the Western world was in ferment. Reactionaries tried vainly to stem the rising tides of nationalism and popular government. Rome, once again a papal state, tried to cling to the old ways, and with all of Italy split up again and squabbling, the task of unification into a single nation seemed impossible. Garibaldi, man of the people and man of the impossible, managed it. In 1849 he abortively seized Rome, but soon lost it to the French who had come to the aid of the Pope. He kept on fighting, and with the Franco-Prussian War draining away French strength, the unification of Italy as a single modern nation was effected under Victor Emmanuel in 1870. In 1871 Rome again became the actual seat of the whole Italian government.

Garibaldi remains in modern Rome, majestic and bronze on a bronze horse, high on top of the Janiculum. (The view of the city from the vantage point of the square around the statue is probably the finest, and on spring and summer nights the Romans flock there to stand in the shadow of Garibaldi and see just how beautiful their city is.) All around him in the park are the marble busts of his heroes who fell in the battle of April 30, 1849, which took place near and on this spot. If you go a few hundred yards and look through the opening of the Porta San Pancrazio you will see how Garibaldi lost the battle and why the park in the Janiculum has so many marble busts. His men poured out of the gate and charged down the long, straight, narrow street directly ahead, with walls on both sides, to try to drive the French from the high ground of the *Villa Doria Pamphili.* The marvel is that they actually made it, took and held the villa briefly. It was a glorious charge, but sheer slaughter every step of the way.

Down the hill a bit from her husband, Anna Garibaldi is immortalized in bronze too. His statue is a noble equestrian, but it is like an action photo, a still to advertise a horse opera. Her horse is galloping away with her at full speed. She holds a baby in one arm and is firing a huge pistol at the enemy with her other hand. She might be Calamity Jane, but somehow the two statues complement each other and give the viewer two sides of the movement.

Victor Emmanuel is memorialized in the huge white marble monument facing the Piazza Venezia. For modern taste it is somewhat overblown and old-fashioned, but tasteful or not, it expresses all the hopes at the time of the unification of Italy of creating once again a Rome imperial.

The man who tried to accomplish just that feat, Benito Mussolini, used to stand on a small balcony of the *Palazzo Venezia* overlooking the square and literally in the shadow of the Victor Emmanuel Monument to harangue enormous crowds with threats and promises. It is true that he made the trains run on time (they still do, without him) and had much to do with the modernization of Rome, the creation of wide boulevards for traffic, modern buildings, lighting, and sanitation. It is also true that his plainclothes secret police, few of them Romans by birth, were everywhere in evidence. But Il Duce had a strong personal following, and even now, he is regretted by a surprising number of Italians.

Indeed, the story of those times is not yet finished. Not far from Garibaldi's monument on the Janiculum is a single isolated marble bust which honors all those, known and unknown, who resisted the

Fascist regime. There are still Romans who carry flowers to that monument by day, and others who seek to deface it by night.

Thirty years ago, the Italians voted in the republic and a visitor can see at a glance the difference between the military dictatorship and the republic in a pleasant way by going to the daily changing of the guard at the President's Palace at four o'clock in the afternoon. When the President of the Republic is in residence (his flag flies from the *Quirinal* on those days), there is a marching band to accompany the ceremony. But this is a changing of the guard like no other. Mothers and nurses bring along the children to see the show, and the children often march along behind the band, imitating it in shrill parody. It is a festive relaxed occasion with no echo of the days of "five million bayonets."

After the war, Italy underwent a tremendous economic expansion which raised the standards of living considerably. However, much of it was superficial with a stress on such things as consumer goods, while basic underlying structures were allowed to stagnate. This situation is now catching up with the country, and Italians are finding themselves victims of multiple ills—unemployment, galloping inflation, corruption at all levels of government, and an incredibly ponderous administrative system, to name only a few. Civil disturbances such as lengthy strikes and even riots are common occurrences in the Italy of the 1970's while, in Rome, governments come and go almost yearly as the difficulties mount up.

Though there is an extremely wide range of political opinion represented in the legislature, political leadership has, for many years, been handled by a center-left coalition. Lately, civil rights issues have been the focus of much legislative activity, and despite the strict Catholic doctrines which have held sway for so long, birth control and divorce were finally legalized. An equal rights law for women was passed in 1975, and the abortion issue is now being raised. But, as the knottier economic problems which Italy shares with the rest of the western world loom larger and larger on the Italian horizon, the radical left is gaining ground markedly, and a brand of Communism, with government control of traditionally private sectors may be the solution the Italians will try next.

Even so short a picture of the long history and background of Rome is sufficient to show that through the ages the people of Rome have seen and known it all. All that has happened to the Western world has, one way or another, happened to Rome and the Romans as well, and it is preserved there for posterity. The people who live in the shadow and under the weight of so much history seem warm and affable and worldly-wise. They are not to be fooled easily by easy slogans and false alarms. They have the confidence of those who have come through.

Rome is living history. And it is our history as members of the Western world as well. The words of the textbooks blur and seem unimportant before the existing facts preserved before your eyes and at your feet in Rome.

CHAPTER *3*

WHAT YOU SHOULD KNOW ABOUT ROME

Climate. Rome's weather is at its best in spring and fall, and fortunately both these seasons are long. In winter the weather is fairly cold (although it rarely goes below freezing), interspersed with periods of mild sunny days, even warm enough for lunching outdoors. The buildings are generally not kept as warm as Americans are used to. They were planned primarily to keep out the summer heat in any case, and you can shiver more indoors than out during the Roman winter. This leads to a practical *fashion note:* in winter Romans wear heavy suits or dresses because of the cold houses, with usually just a light topcoat for outdoor wear. It's just the opposite of the American custom of wearing light clothes indoors and heavy overcoats outside.

In summer, on the other hand, particularly in July and August, Rome can get very hot. Although by sunset, most evenings, there is a cool sea breeze called the *Ponentino,* the summer weather still can make the idea of dutifully trudging around the Forum much less appealing than the prospect of going swimming at the nearest beach.

In spring and fall, however, Rome is a joy. Its days are soft and balmy, with brilliant sunshine spilling over the mellow golden walls. The nights are cool. It rains too, of course, but the rain has a softness about it and the muted colors of Rome glow even under gray skies.

What Clothes to Bring. Rome is full of attractive shops stocking everything you are likely to require in the way of clothing, standard medicines, and cosmetics. It is no longer necessary—if it ever was—to arrive weighed down with extra supplies of cleansing tissues, nylon stockings, aspirin, and lipstick. Electric current varies between 115 and 125 volts but Italian plugs and sockets are different from American ones, so if you bring traveling irons or other electrical equipment, you will have to buy an adaptor for use in Italy.

The Pope greets vast throngs of worshippers from the balcony of St. Peter's

However, with drip-dry clothing so popular among travelers, there is hardly any need for weighty irons, and whatever pressing is necessary can be done at your hotel very quickly and at a reasonable price.

Every guidebook recommends that a woman bring comfortable walking shoes to the Eternal City and its cobblestones. So she should. But she should also have at least one pair of pretty high-heeled shoes for evening. Roman women always dress up to go out to dinner, and in the more fashionable restaurants you will see very chic women indeed. Even at a quiet little *trattoria* you will feel more appropriately dressed if you are not wearing the low-heeled sensible affairs that took you from church to museum to Forum.

In summer, Roman men wear form-fitting shirts, often open to the waist—and it's the rare restaurant that will insist on a tie. But in winter, people feel more comfortable with suits and ties.

Since Rome is a cosmopolitan city you will see people in every style of dress, conservative and bold. A phenomenon of the 1970's is the Roman woman in pants, and even see-throughs, but foreign women who wear provocative outfits are literally asking for trouble from the enterprising Roman men.

Many churches refuse to admit women in sleeveless dresses, so it is a good idea to carry a light sweater or jacket to slip on as you enter. You do not need a hat, however. Bring along a light wrap of some sort to wear in the evenings for dining at an outdoor restaurant, attending the opera at the Baths of Caracalla, or sipping coffee at an outdoor café. The evenings can be surprisingly chilly, even in July. A raincoat is a useful addition to your luggage at any season.

In winter a dinner jacket is essential for men at opening nights of the opera; but for most other occasions a dark blue or gray suit is entirely appropriate.

The Bernini colonnade seen from across St. Peter's Square   *Temple of the Vestals in the Roman Forum*

Modern design as reflected in the framework of the Sports Palace

HOW TO GET AROUND

Rome looks endlessly complicated when you arrive, particularly since streets change their names in mid-course for no apparent reason. But you will find that it is less difficult than it looks and that it is served by a remarkably complete network of buses and trolleys, as well as the new *Metropolitana,* or subway. Most of all, however, Rome is a city for walkers. At every turn there is something to amaze or delight the visitor—from ancient Roman ruins to modern sports arenas, from tranquil shaded cloisters to noisy crowded market places, and from sparkling fountains to sparkling shop windows full of jewelry.

Center of town for most visitors is the Piazza di Spagna, the home of American Express, at the heart of the most fashionable shopping district. The focal point of ancient Rome is the area including the Forum, the Campidoglio, and the Colosseum. The heart of religious Rome is, of course, St. Peter's and the Vatican, on the other side of the Tiber. If you locate these three districts on your map, you will see that most of the other noteworthy sights on your list lie within the triangle between these points.

Buses and trolleys run frequently and cost little. The farè has recently been standardized at 50 lire, and is the same on all lines at all hours, whatever distance you travel. You get on a bus at the back. Keep the ticket you buy from the conductor—an inspector may come around to collect it. A bus stop is called a *fermata,* and each one lists the identifying number of the buses which stop there, besides giving the names of several streets along the route so that you can follow it with your map and decide whether it will take you where you want to go. It's best to avoid the buses during rush hours, when more people are packed in per square inch than you would have dreamed possible. Rush hours in Rome are from 8 to 9 in the morning, 12:30 to 1:30 at midday, 3:30 to 4:30 in the afternoon, and 7:30 to 8:30 in the evening.

Bargain note: to get a good idea of the extent of Rome, take one of the buses which circle the city in either direction. Those that round the city in a clockwise direction are numbered 21, and those that go counterclockwise are numbered 20. Since they follow the same route, it doesn't really matter which way you go. The best place to get a 20 or 21 bus is just outside the Porta Pinciana in Rome, at the end of the Via Veneto. A larger circle around the city can be made on the *Esterna Destra* (number 29) trolley or on a number 30 bus. A good spot to board the ED trolley or the number 30 bus is in front of the Museum of Modern Art. A complete trip on either of these lines will bring you back to your starting point.

Taxis. If you'd rather get about by taxi, you'll find cab stands at most busy street corners and piazzas. Taxis in Rome don't cruise. You can also telephone for a taxi by calling 117; ask for the number of the cab stand nearest you and call it.

Rates are posted in each cab—310 lire for the first 220 meters or two minutes and 30 lire for each additional 220 meters or one minute. A trunk will cost you 50 lire extra and there is a surcharge of 250 lire for trips between 10 P.M. and 7 A.M. Remember, too, that when you telephone for a cab, you pay the fare starting from the cab stand, plus a surcharge of 100 lire. A 100 lire surcharge is applied on Sundays and holidays. For your own protection refuse cabs without meters or those whose drivers want to leave the fare up to you. The standard tip is 10 to 15 percent, which usually means bringing the price up to the nearest 50 or 100 lire.

Horse Cabs. Horse-drawn carriages are a particularly pleasant and leisurely means of seeing part of the city. It is customary to set a price beforehand with the driver, either for the distance you want to go or for the amount of time you expect your outing to last. As an example, a ride from St. Peter's to the Piazza Venezia costs about 4000 lire. Two people would pay a total of 15000 lire for a tour of all Rome. But if the driver's charges seem out of line, you can always refuse to pay until you have discussed the matter with a policeman. In Rome, as elsewhere, there are drivers willing to take advantage of the fact that the passenger happens to be a foreigner who does not speak the language.

Car. If you care to dare the Roman traffic on your own or if you want to use a car to get to surrounding areas such as Tivoli or Ostia Antica, you can rent one (let's say you choose a Fiat 127) for about $7.50 a day plus 12 cents a km. Gasoline is expensive in Italy—now $1.80 a gallon—but if you bring your car and stay in Italy less than 90 days you can get a discount of about 35 per cent by buying gas coupons. Check at the Automobile Club of Italy at

Shadow patterns in the colonnade of the Olympic Stadium

Via Marsala 8. You don't need an International Driver's License—
unless you rent a car, as some rental agencies require them.

Sightseeing. There are several approaches to the problem of sightseeing in Rome. The chief difficulty, most visitors find, is that there
is so much to see in this mammoth and historic city that even a
month's concentrated looking would only scratch the surface. If your
time is limited, a sightseeing tour, or series of tours, by bus is perhaps
the one way you can be sure to see at least the greatest sights in Rome
and its environs. There are a variety of tours available through CIT
(the official Italian company), located at Piazza della Repubblica
64; American Express, at Piazza di Spagna 38; or Thomas Cook,
Via Vittorio Veneto 9/11; or Wagon-Lits, via Boncompagni 25.

If you have more time, or prefer to set your own pace, the best
approach—indeed the only workable one in Rome—is to choose
only what you're really most interested in and not force yourself to
visit something that doesn't appeal to you merely because "everybody" goes to see it. A map of Rome, some walking shoes, and a
spirit of adventure are all you need to explore the innumerable
piazzas, churches, galleries, parks, and fountains of this unique city.
If you saunter through the narrow streets of old Rome, behind the
Piazza Navona, for example, or along the Via Giulia or near the Pantheon, you'll get many unexpected and revealing glimpses of flower-
hung balconies, inner courtyards, and fountains. Here, perhaps more
than in the impressive ruins of antiquity, you will get a little of the
feeling of this city where civilizations have been built on the ruins of
the previous ones for centuries, an ancient city whose vitality seems
to be renewed perpetually.

Out-of-Town Sightseeing.   Rome does not end at the city limits. It is surrounded by scores of unique and interesting places. You should plan to take at least one excursion out of town—to the Castelli Romani (the Alban hill towns) on the shores of volcanic lakes, to Hadrian's Villa with its acres of ruins out in the countryside below Tivoli, to the magnificent fountain display of the Villa d'Este at Tivoli, and to the extensive remains of the old seaport of Rome at Ostia Antica. All of these are less than an hour's drive from the center of town, and any of the leading travel agencies have regular daily tours to them. A little farther away are the Etruscan tombs at Cerveteri and the astonishingly beautiful frescoed tombs at Tarquinia. But there is much you'll want to see along the way, and for this trip you may decide to hire a car.

Air Travel.   Rome's airport is about forty minutes' drive from the center of town, and the airlines maintain regular transportation service from the Air Terminal at Via Giolitti 36. The airport is officially called the aeroporto Leonardo Da Vinci, but is often referred to as Fiumicino, the name of the nearest little town.

   Most of the world's airlines have offices in Rome. The abbreviated list below includes only the larger international lines. For others, consult the phone book.

   Air France, Via Vittorio Veneto 89. Tel. 478.941.
   Alitalia, Via Bissolati 13. Tel. 5454 or 4688.
   British Airways, Via Bissolati 48-54. Tel. 486.494.
   KLM, Via Barberini 97. Tel. 489.121.
   Pan American World Airways, Via Bissolati 46. Tel. 475.4841.
   Sabena, Via Barberini 111. Tel. 475.0241.
   Swissair, Via Bissolati 4. Tel. 460.652.
   TWA, Via Barberini 59. Tel. 475.1141.

Interior of the Pantheon; Ceiling of Basilica of S. Maria Maggiore

Cloister of the Basilica of San Lorenzo al Verano

Tourist Information. If you need help in planning a sightseeing tour, in figuring out how to get from one city to another, or in deciding what parts of Italy to visit, you can get sound advice, up-to-date information, and a great deal of literature from the government tourist bureau (ENIT), Via Marghera 2 (tel. 495.0601). For specific information about Rome and the province of Lazio, visit the provincial tourist association (EPT), which maintains offices at Via Parigi 11 (tel. 461.851), at the main railroad station, and at both branches of the airport. In addition, the Rome City Office for Tourism has an office at Via Tomacelli 107 (tel. 671.060). The American Express, Piazza di Spagna 38, and CIT, Piazza della Repubblica 64, can provide useful information.

ENTERTAINMENT

Music and Theaters. Rome's music season starts in October and continues into June. There are orchestra concerts, chamber music and outstanding soloists at the Pius XII Auditorium on Via della Conciliazione, the Eliseo Theater on Via Nazionale, the National Academy of St. Cecilia on Via dei Greci, and the Aula Magna of the University of Rome. The opera season starts the day after Christmas at the Rome opera house and continues until late spring.

In summer, opera is given outdoors at the imposing Baths of Caracalla, and outdoor concerts are presented in the Basilica di Massenzio in the Forum. These are both magnificent settings, evocative of ancient Rome, and a musical performance in either is an unusual experience. There is a minor opera season in late spring and early fall at the Eliseo Theater.

The theater in Rome sticks largely to revivals of the classics, including Shakespeare in Italian, and Italian versions of American, British, or French successes; only a few new Italian plays are given each year. Handsome musical revues are mounted at the Sistina Theater during the winter; and you can enjoy the singing, dancing, and lavish costumes even though the language may escape you. In summer, classic plays are performed outdoors in the lovely Greek Theater at Ostia Antica.

Tickets to concerts, operas, plays, and sports events must be purchased at individual theaters or through your concierge.

Sports. Soccer is by far the most popular spectator sport in Rome—as it is throughout Italy. From September to May you can see a game any Sunday afternoon at the Olympic Stadium. Both home teams, Rome and Lazio, are formidable competitors, as are most visiting opponents.

For the most part, tennis is confined to the many sports clubs in Rome. There are, however, also public courts near the Villa Borghese and in the EUR section. For golf, there is the Acqua Santa Golf Club, where guest privileges are available.

The nearest skiing is some 65 miles from Rome at Monte Terminillo, a 5,000-foot resort. You can either drive out along the Via Salaria or get there by early-morning bus service. Weekdays are best; on Sundays the runs are likely to be crowded.

Beaches. The beach resorts of *Ostia* and *Fregene* are less than an hour away by car, and Ostia and nearby *Castelfusano* can be reached by train from the Stazione Termini. The best-known bathing establishments at Castelfusano are Kursaal (with pool), Sporting Beach, and Gambrinus. If Ostia's dark sands aren't what you are looking for, take the bus to Fregene, where the "in" places are Toni's, Albos, and La Nave. The Villa dei Pini is an excellent pension in Fregene with serene gardens under the pines and good food. Gina's restaurant in the Fisherman's Village there has superb seafood.

Pools. Try the Foro Italico, the EUR, and on the outskirts of Rome the roof pool of the Caesar Augustus Hotel. The Excelsior has Turkish baths.

Sulphur-water swimming pools at Bagni di Tivoli in the pleasant, tree-shaded spa, are reputedly health-giving, and—once you get used to the sulphur smell—refreshing. The *piscina riservata* (reserved pool) is preferable.

Newspapers. The Rome *Daily American* and the *International Herald Tribune,* published in Paris, are available at most large newsstands. You can also find a number of British newspapers, particularly at the newsstands in the Via Veneto or Piazza di Spagna neighborhood. American news magazines arrive promptly by airmail; other magazines are at least three weeks old.

SOME QUICK FACTS

The Roman Schedule. Italy is blessed with numerous holidays during which stores and offices are closed. (For a list, see the Holiday Guide to Italy.) In addition, many businesses shut up shop for a period varying from two days to as much as a month in August. August 15, *Ferragosto,* marks the beginning of the national holiday period, and from a few days before the holiday until nearly the end of the month Rome is far less active and busy than usual. Conse-

The Caffe Greco—one of Rome's oldest cafes

quently August is by no means the best month for shopping, although you can go sightseeing, listen to outdoor concerts and opera, and enjoy the nearby beaches then as well as or better than at other times.

Summer store hours in Rome are from 9 A.M. to 1 P.M. and from 4 P.M. to 8 (except for grocery stores, which reopen at 5:30 P.M.). The rest of the year, morning store hours are the same, but stores reopen in the afternoon at 4:00 and close at 7:30. Banks are open from 9 to 1:30, but closed all afternoon. Certain banks are also open Saturday mornings from 8:30 to 11:00. Stores also close for half a day every week but the closings are not uniform, and you should check before going out to shop. Food stores close Saturday afternoons in summer, and Thursday afternoons in winter.

Most Roman museums are open from 9 to 1 and from 3 or 4 to 6 on weekdays and are closed on Sunday afternoons. A few remain open straight through till 3 or 4 on weekdays. Many are closed on Mondays. The Vatican Museum is open from 9 A.M. to 2 P.M. and is closed all day on Sundays (except for the last Sunday of each month) and holidays. In summer some museums have regularly scheduled evening hours. Barber shops (except for hotel barbers) are open Sunday mornings and closed all day Mondays, but hairdressers are closed Sundays and open Mondays. There is probably a reason for this intriguing variety.

Romans go home at one o'clock, have lunch, and then pull down the shades and go to bed for their siesta. The idea is well worth trying. Particularly in summer, when the midday heat is intense, you will find yourself much relaxed after a rest of an hour or so. Refreshed and energized you emerge when it is cooler to continue your sightseeing or shopping.

Stazione Termini, Rome's striking modern station

Medical Care. In case of need, the American embassy will supply you with a recommended list of English-speaking doctors and dentists. Salvator Mundi, an international hospital where English is spoken, is at Viale delle Mura Gianicolensi (tel. 580.0141). For emergency ambulance service, call the Red Cross, Via Pacinotti 18 (tel. 555.666). First aid is available at the railroad station and, of course, all city hospitals are prepared to give emergency treatment.

A drugstore is called a *farmacia*. But remember, in Rome, drugstores do not deal in general merchandise; they sell only medicines and toilet goods. Lepitit International Pharmacy, Via del Corso 418 (tel. 679.1347) also sells many American cosmetic products. Most drugstores are closed at night, but your hotel *concierge* will know where you can find one open. Among those regularly open at night are: Carlo Erba, Via del Corso 145 (tel. 679.0866); Garinei, Piazza San Silvestro 31 (tel. 679.3198); Farmacia Internationale, Piazza Risorgimento 44 (tel. 351.591).

Piazza Esedra and, to the right, the Baths of Diocletion

Churches and Religious Services.   Since Rome, the center of the
Catholic world, has some 400 churches, you will have no difficulty in
locating one that you like. But the city is not so well provided with
churches of other faiths. Here is a list, including Catholic churches
with services in English, which may be useful.

All Saints' (Church of England), Via del Babuino 153b.
Christian Science Society, Via dei Giardini 42.
Methodist, Via Banco di Santo Spirito 3.
St. Andrew's (Scottish Presbyterian), Via XX Settembre 7.
Santa Maria dell'Umiltà (American Catholic), Via dell'Umiltà.
St. Patrick's (English-speaking Catholic), Via Boncompagni 33.
St. Paul's (American Episcopal), Via Napoli 58.
San Silvestro (English-speaking Catholic), Piazza San Silvestro.
Santa Susanna (American Catholic), Piazza San Bernardo.
Synagogue (Jewish), Lungotevere dei Cenci.

Azaleas in full bloom along the Spanish Steps

Papal Audiences.   Information about arranging papal audiences can
be obtained through the North American College, Via dell'Umiltà
30 (tel. 678.0580). During the latter part of the summer, the Pope
moves to his summer residence at Castel Gandolfo, in the Alban
Hills about fifteen miles from Rome. Audiences are also regularly
held there.

Telephones. Most public telephones are located in bars. You will find them by looking for the yellow sign with a telephone on it posted outside. To make a local call, ask the cashier for a slug (*gettone*) and insert it in the slot above the phone *with the single groove facing front in a vertical position.* Then dial your number. When you hear someone answer, press the button next to the slot to let the slug drop into the box. If you fail to push the button, the person you are calling won't be able to hear you although you will hear him. If there is no answer, or the line is busy, you just remove the slug. For a new type of pay phone, you must push a red button to recover your slug.

Long-distance calls must be made either from a private phone or from the telephone company offices. There is one at Via della Mercede (open all night), next to the central post office. For information, dial 12. For the correct time, dial 16. To report a fire, dial 44.4.44. For the police, dial 113.

To dictate cables and express telegrams, dial 186. It is usually easier, however, particularly if you are sending a wire in English, to go to the main telegraph office in the San Silvestro post office.

For train information and to reserve seats, dial 4775. (Berths in sleeping cars must be reserved through a travel agency or at the *Termini Station.*)

Flea Market. Every Sunday an enormous quantity of secondhand (to put it mildly) goods is heaped on the Via Portuense beyond the Porta Portese in Trastevere. In the midst of incredible quantities of junk, there is sometimes an article worth buying—for those sharp-eyed enough to spot it and vociferous enough in bargaining to bring the price down to somewhere near where it ought to be. Be wary, however, of so-called Etruscan objects; they're not authentic (if they were, they wouldn't be at the market), and of antiques which are supposed to be of rare value. On the other hand, you may well pick up a decorative curio, a bit of old jewelry, or something else that you will enjoy almost as much as you do prowling through the market itself.

At Piazza Fontanella di Borghese, in the center of town, you will find old prints, books, copper utensils, and various kinds of bric-a-brac for sale in a small open market every day.

USEFUL ADDRESSES

American Academy	Via Angelo Masina 5 (tel. 588.653)
American Chamber of Commerce for Italy	Via Lombardia 40 (tel. 475.4540)
American Consulate	Via Vittorio Veneto 121
American Embassy	Via Vittorio Veneto 119 (tel. 4674 for both)
American Express	Piazza di Spagna 38 (tel. 688.751)

Automobile Club of Italy	Via Marsala 8 (tel. 4998)
CIT	Piazza della Repubblica 64 (tel. 479.041)
Cook, Thomas	Via Vittorio Veneto 9/11 (tel. 479.441)
Hertz	Via Sallustiana 28 (tel. 476.741)
Sabastianelli Car Rental	Via Flaminia 310 (tel. 393.936)
Lost and Found Bureau	Via Nicolo Bettoni 1 (tel. 581.6040)
Medical Service	
RED CROSS AMBULANCE SERVICE	Via Pacinotti 18 (tel. 555.666)
SALVATOR MUNDI INTERNATIONAL HOSPITAL	Viale delle Mura Gianicolensi 67 (tel. 580.0141)
POLICLINICO A. GEMELLI	Via Pineta Sacchetti 526 (tel. 38.75)
BAMBINO GESÙ (children's hospital)	Piazza Sant'Onofrio 4 (tel. 657.451)
North American College	Via dell'Umiltà 30 (tel. 678.0580)
Police Headquarters	Via S. Vitale 15 (tel. 461.010 or 479.161)
Emergency police calls	(tel. 113)
Post Office	Piazza San Silvestro (tel. 180)
Telegraph and Cable Office	Post Office. Piazza San Silvestro
Telephone Office	Via della Mercede, next to central post office. Open all night.
Touring Club of Italy	7/A Via Ovidio (tel. 388.602)
Tourist Information	
ENIT	Via Marghera 2 (tel. 495.0601)
EPT	Via Parigi 11 (tel. 461.851) and at the main railroad station (tel. 465.461)
ROME CITY OFFICE FOR TOURISM	Via Tomacelli 107 (tel. 671.060)
United States Information Service Library (USIS)	Via Veneto 62 (tel. 4674)
Wagon-Lits	Via Boncompagni 25 (tel. 476.651)

CHAPTER 4

WHAT TO SEE IN ROME

I: THE HIGHLIGHTS

There are some things that just have to be seen in Rome because, like Mt. Everest, they "are there." But whether you are in Rome for a few days or a long leisurely visit, you are sure to find there is just too much to see and do. Even the basic things which you will feel you must not miss make a formidable (and debated) list. The plain truth is that unless you want your stay in Rome to remain in your memory as a kind of vague, uneasy, footsore, and eye-straining experience, choices will have to be made. Some things will have to be seen and done at the expense of others which will just have to remain, perhaps, for another day.

Rome defies organizing. The usual guidebook to the city, and there have been many, is arranged according to the sections of the city or by tours which describe the points of interest between one known landmark and another. This is all well and good if you merely want to know where you are and where you are going. But in practice it proves to be an indiscriminate and exhausting way to see the city. It's a little like trying to map the open sea.

Perhaps the best thing to do right away is to get a sense of the whole city by spending a few minutes with the map and taking a guided tour or two. You will find that Rome really covers a rather small and compact area as great cities go. Many well-planned tours of the city are available through the various tourist agencies. They flit about, swift as bees among flowers, briefly touching the high spots and moving on. The jokes of the guides are sometimes a little threadbare, and you may occasionally be embarrassed by the inevitable and inane questions of some of your fellow countrymen, but you will

Massive ruins of the Baths of Caracalla

come back from the guided tour with a real sense of the whole city as a unit, a place in itself, and with the likelihood that you won't get lost or befuddled on your own excursions.

Another, cheaper way to see the city, the *Circolare* Buses, has already been mentioned in Chapter 3, THINGS TO KNOW ABOUT ROME. The trip takes from three-quarters of an hour to an hour and costs about 8 cents (50 lire). It's a pleasant orientation, and you are likely to encounter English-speaking companions, British tourists who have to watch their pennies. The ultimate in economy—and possibly in pleasure—would be to take some of the very fascinating walking tours of Rome described in the readable but informative *Companion Guide to Rome* by Georgina Masson, sold all over the city.

Of course for the lucky ones who don't have to be concerned about costs, there are private guided tours by rented car, cab, or horse-drawn carriage.

After you've acquired at least a vague sense of the shape of the city and some rough notion of where things are, the fun begins. You are ready to decide what to see and when to see it. The latter is an important consideration, for things have a way of opening and closing at odd hours, without relation to each other or to the rest of Rome. There are, for example, some churches and even a few museums which are open one day a year. The only way to be absolutely sure of the hours, which change from year to year and even from week to week, is to check with any one of the reputable tourist agencies.

This chapter is intended to help you make the basic choices and begin your visit in Rome with a minimum of strain and pain.

CHURCHES

Rome is a city of churches, nearly four hundred in all. Some of them were built recently, and others, centuries old themselves, stand on the foundations of places where the Apostles Peter and Paul preached. Most of them are day-to-day working parish churches, but there are a few which are now no more than museums. Some are always open, others are open seldom, if at all. If you had a lifetime to devote to it, you could never know them all.

The first church of Rome, not in time, but clearly in unquestioned importance, is **St. Peter's**.

It is no accident that from whatever direction you approach St. Peter's, you must enter through the *Piazza San Pietro.* Designed by the Roman genius of the Baroque, Bernini, this magnificent piazza was intended to be part of the whole experience of St. Peter's, to serve as a preparation for, and introduction to, the great church. There are two plain leaping jets, fountains built on the design of Carlo Maderna in the 17th century. These are the first impression before the façade of St. Peter's. Simple, yet amazingly forceful, these fountains seem to express with convincing clarity the monumental and powerful simplicity of the Christian faith.

Bernini had an enormous area to work with. He also had some major problems, not the least of which was the functional one of designing a space to accommodate upwards of the half a million people who gather there for important occasions and celebrations. His solution is a masterpiece. He enclosed the space of the piazza with a colonnade—two slim porticos supported by 284 columns. Without reducing the space of the piazza, this enclosure makes it *seem* smaller than it is, thus not detracting in any way from the monumental impression of the church itself. Each arm of the colonnade is composed of four parallel arms of columns; the two major arms are laid out along the circumference of an ellipse, and the columns are placed behind one another on lines drawn from the two *foci* of the ellipse. This means that if you stand at the north focus, you have the illusion of only one row of columns in the colonnade nearest you. But turn and look behind you, and you see all four rows of the south colonnade in apparent disorder. The opposite effect happens if you stand at the south focus and look the other way. The final effect is of a curious and profound tension between reason (the neat geometry you see ahead) and faith (what you can't see, but imagine behind you). Bernini seems to have had in mind man's perplexity, the visible need for the answer provided by the great church standing there. In the center of the piazza is an *obelisk* topped by a triumphant cross. The only one in Rome which has never been overthrown, this slender shaft of stone was once silent witness to the tortures and martyrdoms which Nero inflicted on Christians in his Circus.

Perhaps the most subtle and amazing feat of Bernini was his handling of the pavement of the square. It looks level. It is not, as you can learn by kneeling and looking closely. No matter how huge and compact the crowd in the piazza, no one is ever excluded from a view of St. Peter's. It is as if Bernini had designed an experience especially for each individual among the million who may (and do) pack the square. The result is that the enormous crowds which gather there as a matter of course on, say, Easter Sunday, are quiet, easily handled, and in a proper mood for devotions. Only in our own time have we begun to discover just how thoughtful the extravagant and talented Bernini was. It is no wonder he was a favorite of Popes and great men. The Piazza San Pietro is as satisfying and complex an aesthetic experience as Rome has to offer.

St. Peter's is the largest church in Christendom; its façade, designed by Carlo Maderna and completed fifty years before Bernini's colonnade, is all that it ought to be—truly monumental. The curious thing is, though, that since everything is proportionate, related, and balanced in the best Renaissance manner, it does not *seem* to be nearly as big as it really is. It is no help to know that the columns are ninety-two feet high or that the tiny statues of Christ and the Apostles on top are really more than eighteen feet tall. It needs the human figure for true perspective. If you look up to the dome, the chances are that you will see visitors looking out from the "lantern" on top of the dome. Then the surprise is achieved. The whole building seems to grow enormous before your eyes. The great *central door,* a remnant of an older basilica of St. Peter's, is decorated with bas-reliefs depicting, among other things, the martyrdoms of St. Peter and St. Paul. A little to the right is a closed door, the Porta Santa, which is only opened during celebrations in a jubilee year.

When you enter the central door, you find an interior quite as large-scaled in its details as the façade. And as with the façade, its size is difficult to comprehend because of the perfect relationship of the parts. But if you look around (and up) a bit you are very likely to see the *sampietrini*—workmen who maintain the church and who once lived on the roof of St. Peter's—at their continual job of cleaning and repairing. They work on high ladders and scaffolds and swing like spiders on a great length of rope from column to column. When you see one of them high against the side of the interior, you again become aware of the true size of this enormous edifice.

Along the sides of the long nave and its parallel aisles are more decorations made by Bernini. Huge statues seem to lunge out of the niches where he placed them. The light of the dome falls in theatrical shafts on the *High Altar.* Bernini helped to emphasize this focus of devotional attention by the design of his *Baldachino* over the High Altar. It too is a characteristically colossal structure, ninety-five feet high, made of cast bronze and elaborately ornamented with figures, branches and laurels, tassels and scrolls. It almost seems as if rigid bronze had been made as soft and pliable as plaster and moulded into these intricate figures.

Sunlit fountain before St. Peter's; Interior of dome of St. Peter's

Majestic sweep of the colonnade around St. Peter's square

The stones and materials used in the church are both historic and symbolic. For example, the bronze which Bernini worked into the twisted forms of the Baldachino came from the pagan Pantheon; the High Altar—at which only the Pope may celebrate the Mass—is a block of Greek marble from the Forum of Nerva. The chapels are filled with works of art, paintings, mosaics, and sculpture by the great names of Italian art. One of the most beautiful, the *Capella della Pietà,* near the Porta Santa centers around Michelangelo's *Pietà,* a shining, deeply moving piece of marble, and the only piece the sculptor ever signed. You can see his name carved in the ribbon which falls across the left shoulder of the Virgin.

But for all the magnificent art which it houses, St. Peter's is neither a museum nor an art gallery. It is a busy working church. If you are in Rome when there is a Pontifical Mass, or for that matter any Mass at St. Peter's, you will see the great church as it was meant to be seen, brilliant with color and ceremony and crowded with throngs of the devout and curious. The Italians are by nature so inherently curious themselves that they would never dream of objecting to those of other faiths who are there only to see the sights. It is exactly what they would do under the same circumstances.

There are really three levels to St. Peter's. The *Dome* can be reached by stairway or elevator. It offers a spectacular view of the city and, directly below, the deft geometry of the piazza. Then there is the world beneath the church, the *Vatican Grottoes.* Small groups are led down by guides to a level where recent excavations have disclosed an ancient necropolis. It begins as pre-Christian, but as you move through the ancient passageways and past the tombs, Christian inscriptions start to appear. The climax of this tour is a view of what historical and circumstantial evidence indicates is the tomb of the Apostle Peter, on which the original church was built.

One of the great basilicas of Rome is **St. John Lateran**. It is the actual cathedral church of Rome and of the whole Catholic world. Under the Lateran Treaty of 1929, it was declared and remains extra-territorial. The piazza before it, Piazza di Porta San Giovanni, is huge and spacious, but it is not, like Bernini's, designed exclusively as an approach to the church. Traffic crosses and recrosses the area, and the church stands to one side. In the center of the piazza rises the *Obelisk of the Lateran,* the oldest object in Rome, thought to have been carved by the Egyptians in 1449 B.C. The façade of St. John Lateran, simple and monumental, is topped by sixteen colossal statues of Christ and the Apostles and saints. You can see these statues from many parts of Rome, and, like the Victor Emmanuel Monument, they serve excellently as fixed points for your navigations. On St. John's Day the piazza is packed with thousands of people in carnival mood. They fire skyrockets and roman candles at the defenseless statues—a solid hit brings good luck—and the statues bring luck to many.

The interior of St. John Lateran is rich with objects of art and history. The *Papal Altar,* in a central space at the end of the long nave, contains many holy relics, including the skulls of Peter and Paul and a piece of Peter's wooden altar table. The *cloister* adjoining the church is one of the most beautiful in Rome, rivaling the smaller and more intimate cloister of *Quattro Coronati* in its design for peaceful meditation and prayer.

Next to the church is the **Lateran Palace**. Once the palace of the Popes, now the *Vicariate of Rome*, it housed until recently three museums: the *Museum of Pagan Antiquities*, the *Christian Museum*, and the *Missionary Museum*. These three collections have been transferred to the *Vatican Museum*. The Pagan Museum is filled with statues, archeological fragments, and a few fine mosaics from classical times. The Christian Museum, probably the most significant and unique of the three, contains objects found in the catacombs and a collection of Christian sarcophagi and inscriptions from the 2nd to the 5th century. The Missionary Museum, founded only thirty years ago, displays works from the distant and exotic regions where Catholic missionaries have labored. Among the most interesting examples are those in which native arts have been adapted to sacred subjects.

Basilica of St. John Lateran

On the Esquiline Hill, facing the Piazza S. Maria Maggiore, stands the church of **S. Maria Maggiore**, like St. Peter's and St. John Lateran, one of the four patriarchal basilicas of Rome, and like them, extra-territorial. The façade, built originally in the 12th century, was badly tampered with in the 18th century and now seems large and undistinguished. But the interior is especially noteworthy because of its 5th-century mosaics, the best in Rome, and its early frescoes. The coffered ceiling is interesting historically, as well as artistically. It was gilded with the first load of gold Columbus brought back from the New World. S. Maria is the only one of the four great patriarchal churches in which the basic Roman basilica form has been preserved, and the extreme and classic simplicity enhances the richness of the mosaics, the frescoes, and the ceiling.

About a mile or so beyond the Porta Paola is **St. Paul's Outside the Walls**, the fourth of the patriarchal basilicas, second in size only to St. Peter's. And just as St. Peter's was built above the tomb of St. Peter, so St. Paul's stands on the site of the tomb of Paul. The interior has a unique and dazzling richness. The great rows of granite columns, the shimmering white and gold of the ceiling, the rare and beautiful marbles which line the exterior, are all caught and reflected in the high polish of the marble floor. The *Chapel of the Crucifix,* one of many in the church, is of special interest, for it was here that the crucifix on the altar spoke to St. Bridget in 1370. Here also St. Ignatius de Loyola took the formal oaths which established the Jesuits as a religious order. In the cloister, a fine, small one from an old Benedictine convent, roses bloom in endless profusion.

Anyone interested in the great churches dedicated to the Apostles of Rome will not miss **S. Pietro in Vincoli**, only a few blocks from the Colosseum, in the center of the city. Founded in 442 as a shrine dedicated to preserving the chains with which Herod bound St. Peter in Jerusalem, it is splendidly adorned and decorated. But its single unforgettable masterpiece is a part of a great unfinished work—the seated figure of *Moses,* which Michelangelo made to adorn the *Tomb of Julius II.* Long-bearded, stern, and powerful, the very personification of justice and the law of the Old Testament, Moses appears about to spring to his feet and pass judgment. The magnificent figure, one of Michelangelo's finest, seems perfectly suited to the spirit of the shrine.

Many of the most important and impressive churches in Rome are dedicated to the Virgin. The first to be so dedicated, and one of the earliest official churches in the city, **S. Maria in Trastevere**, rises above a piazza of the same name in the fashionable and very picturesque section of Trastevere. Built in the 3rd century and remodeled in 1140, it has been very little changed since. It is best known for its mosaics and especially for the one on the exterior, a 12th-century representation of the Madonna which adorns the façade. S. Maria in Trastevere is the favorite church of many long-time American residents of Rome, who, particularly during the great celebrations of Christmas and Easter Sunday, prefer its pristine simplicity and piety to the extravagance of other, better-known churches.

Another of the famous churches dedicated to the Virgin is **S. Maria in Aracoeli**, handsomely situated atop the Capitoline Hill and adjacent to the Capitol. The long stairway leading to the church from the street below is favored by pilgrims, but less pious or vigorous visitors simply walk over from the Capitol. The façade of simple, austere brick dates from the 13th century. Earlier pagan temples stood on the same site. One of them is thought to have been the *Temple of the Unknown God,* erected by Augustus when he heard from an oracle a vague prophecy of a triumphant Christ. The dim interior, lit only by shafts of light slanting through slits in the brick walls, seems bare. As a result, the eye turns directly to the candles of the altar. But there are great works of art here, notably some frescoes by Pinturicchio, said to be among his finest works. One chapel contains the wooden figure of the *Infant Christ,* said to have been carved by angels from an olive tree in the Garden of Gethsemane. The figure is believed to have healing powers, and at any hour of the day or night may be carried by the Friars who protect it to the home of a sick or disabled person who has asked to see it. S. Maria is especially festive during the Christmas season, when small children come to recite poems in honor of the Christ Child; often, even during the Mass, bagpipers down from the mountains of Abruzzi invade the church with their shrill music.

Just below the Pincian Hill, and looking across the wide and gracious Piazza del Popolo, is **S. Maria del Popolo,** which has more than a fair share of great art in its chapels. Represented are Pinturicchio, Bramante, Raphael, Lorenzetto, Bernini, and there are two paintings in the chapel just to the left of the choir by Caravaggio, an artist who is just now beginning to receive proper critical attention and appreciation. There is something of a sense of discovery involved in finding two Caravaggios in one church. (Those especially interested in Caravaggio will want to see two other seldom-visited churches which boast Caravaggio paintings: **S. Agostino** on the tiny Via di S. Ago-

Michelangelo's Moses *in S. Pietro in Vincoli; S. Maria in Cosmedin*

Interior, Basilica of St. Paul's Outside the Walls

stino, not far from the Piazza Navona—which also has a Raphael —and **S. Luigi dei Francesi**, near the Palazzo Madama, which has three.)

But with all its fine art, S. Maria del Popolo is very much a working parish church. Here art is used, as well as appreciated; for the chapels are all dark, and next to the light switch in each is a small mite box for charitable donations. For a few *lire* given to charity, you can snap on a light and have a painting by Raphael spring to life. The floor of the church, once used as a burial place, is now almost covered with inscribed stones. You can hardly turn in any direction without stepping on the grave of some famous nobleman or ecclesiastical dignitary.

S. Maria Degli Angeli, which stands conveniently facing the Piazza Esedra, is of interest for two reasons. First, it is actually a hall—the best preserved one—of the *Baths of Diocletian,* simply appropriated and transformed into a Christian church. Secondly, the remodeling, done by Michelangelo, was the last work ever accomplished by that great genius. It is a tradition that the vaulted halls of the Baths were built by enslaved Christians who were killed when the job was finished. It seems fitting that later Christians were able to put their labor to use in a church.

On the Vicolo della Pace near Piazza Navona, is **S. Maria della Pace**, famous for its paintings by Raphael—the four Prophets and the Sibyls—and for its second chapel which was designed by Michelangelo. It is a small church, which you must enter from the side through a cloister designed by Bramante. In our times it is a favorite wedding church among the young Romans, and it has become a custom for the young couple to return on their first anniversary to offer thanks to the Virgin.

Not even the briefest listing of churches dedicated to the Virgin would be complete without mention of **S. Maria in Cosmedin** on the Piazza della Bocca della Verità. Built in the 6th century and restored in the 12th, it is a perfect example of the Roman church of the Middle Ages. Its *campanille,* pure Romanesque and a hundred feet high, is a familiar landmark. Under the open portico of the church is the *Bocca della Verità,* the Mouth of Truth, a marble face whose open mouth is supposed to snap shut when the hand of a liar is placed in it. How dependable it is, no one knows. You'll remember that in *Roman Holiday* Audrey Hepburn tried it, told a white lie and got away without being bitten. The interior of the church is dark and simple—twelve ancient marble columns, taken from Roman buildings, dividing the nave, and a rare, raised choir like that of S. Clemente. Especially interesting is the luxurious pavement of colored stones, like an abstract mosaic, called *opus cosmatescum.* In the absence of stained-glass windows (which are very rare in Rome, and indeed, in all of Italy), this richly colored floor catches the light and mints it into coins of pure color. The sacristy of the church has a mosaic, *The Adoration of the Magi,* which is one of the very few relics of the old St. Peter's. And one thing more: on Valentine's Day the skull of St. Valentine is exhibited here, crowned with fresh roses.

Even for the visitor with a limited time in Rome, there are three other churches which are worth a visit. Not famous for works of art or for any singular splendor, they are, nevertheless, among the most important churches of the city. They were founded by the Emperor Constantine, the first great Christian Emperor. Of the seven basilicas he created to celebrate his faith, these three remain, much restored and repaired, but still somehow retaining the spirit in which they were originally erected. They are: **S. Croce in Gerusalemme**, erected to preserve a part of the true cross brought to Rome from Jerusalem by the Emperor's mother, St. Helena; **S. Lorenzo Fuori Le Mura**, noted now for its fine 13th-century frescoes and its *cosmati* floor (like that of S. Maria in Cosmedin), dating from the 12th century; and **S. Agnes Fuori Le Mura**, often singled out for the beauty of its wooden ceiling and ciborium.

The Sistine Room of the Vatican Library

MUSEUMS

A tour of the Roman churches begins at the source and heart—St. Peter's. And any tour of the museums should really begin at the same place, at the adjoining VATICAN MUSEUM. This is a collective name for many related and connected museums in the Vatican. It is un-equaled in the city by any standard, quantity or quality, and—though this may possibly be debatable—it is in an over-all sense unequaled anywhere in the world. Its sheer enormity is forbidding. It is obvious that a dozen day-long trips would not let you see every-thing, and it is equally unlikely that in a lifetime you could *know* everything that is displayed there. The best (and only) way to see the Vatican and still preserve your feet and eyes, is to select the section or sections of the museum that most interest you, and once there, with the help of the little handbooks that all the museums of Rome have to offer, to select again. Before you plunge in, take a few min-utes at the beginning to decide what particular things you most want to see—and then, in spite of all distractions, stick to your plan.

To begin with, there is the **Vatican Picture Gallery**, fifteen large public rooms with 460 paintings. This enormous collection includes famous works by such masters as Fra Angelico, Leonardo da Vinci, Raphael, Titian, Caravaggio, Pinturicchio, Perugino, Van Dyck, and many others. Here, then, is the first test of your resolution. Don't try to see everything; concentrate on the works of a few painters you know and appreciate.

Then there are the various Museums of Antiquities, which together make up the largest collection of ancient sculpture in the world. The Museums of Antiquities are broken down, roughly, into four main parts: (1) the **Museo Pio-Clementino**, (2) the **Etruscan Museum**, (3) the **Egyptian Museum**, and (4) the **Chiaramonti Gallery**. Though the Etruscan and Egyptian museums are good, their contents are equaled and even excelled elsewhere. The museum of the Villa Giulia is superior for Etruscan items, and anyway it isn't likely that you came to Rome to study the Egyptians. The other two sections contain works of classical sculpture unsurpassed elsewhere in the world. You enter through the *Hall of the Greek Cross* and come almost at once into the *Round Hall,* designed in imitation of the Pantheon and decorated with the largest mosaic in the museum. It is a room of "big" things; the *Hercules,* the largest bronze statue ever found, and the colossal *Antinoüs,* created to honor the friend and favorite of Hadrian. The next most important room is the *Gallery of Statues,* with a great range and variety of classical figures. The *Cab-inet of Masks,* which takes its name from the theatrical floor mosaic found in Hadrian's Villa, has a few fine pieces well displayed; most important is the *Venus of Cnidos,* best extant copy of the famous nude by Praxiteles. In the *Court of Belvedere* are two of the most famous of all pieces of classical sculpture: the *Laocoön,* father and two sons writhing in a death grip of marble serpents, and the incomparable *Apollo Belvedere,* the finest example of ancient Greek sculpture (4th century B.C.) in the museum. If your interest is aroused, you can see a great deal more of classical sculpture in the adjoining **Chiaramonti Gallery** and the **New Wing**. But, if you are on a time budget, only at the expense of the greater works still to come.

Connected with the **Vatican Library**, that enormous repository of books and manuscripts that has never yet been fully catalogued and is not likely to be in this century, are the **Museum of Pagan Antiquities**, a small museum of classical things (and a marvelous coin collection) created in the 18th century; the **Sistine Hall**, with a great number of Greek and Roman manuscripts under glass; and the varied **Museum of Christian Art**. The latter leads inevitably—and swiftly —to a celebrated section of the Vatican, the **Borgia Rooms**, six rooms which were decorated by one of the finest of Italian painters, Pinturicchio, and contain a lavish display of his frescoes. A stairway from the first of these rooms leads to still another unmatched aesthetic experience—the **Raphael Rooms**. These four large rooms contain, walls and ceiling, the masterworks of Raphael, executed for Pope Julius II, who will also be remembered for recognizing the genius of Michelangelo and Bramante and putting them to work for the Church.

But it is the **Sistine Chapel** that must and should draw everyone who comes to Rome. The walls are magnificently frescoed by such masters as Botticelli, Pinturicchio, and Perugino, but this room is Michelangelo's alone, dominated and possessed once and for all by the ceiling frescoes he painted in the four fantastic years of 1508–1512. The paintings illustrate episodes from Genesis, from the Creation through the life of Noah. In the lunettes over the windows he painted the prophets and the Sibyls, overlooking the Old Testament events and prophesying the coming of Christ. More than twenty years after he had finished the ceiling, Michelangelo returned to paint *The Last Judgment* on the Altar Wall. The artist had no doubt whatever of his genius, for without hesitation he demanded that the windows be walled up and that two earlier frescoes by Perugino be destroyed. He also found a way to revenge himself on those who objected to his art. The Master of Ceremonies to Pope Paul II had protested against the nudity of some of his figures; Michelangelo simply included his face in Hell, graced with ass's ears.

In natural awe and wonder at this miraculous display of one man's genius, we often forget that this small chapel still serves its function as the private chapel of the Pope and as the meeting place of the Conclave of Cardinals. Testimony to the latter function is the small stove with the slender metal flue which stands by the wall, where as millions remember, the ballots of the Cardinals are burned in Papal elections. Thousands stand in the piazza below looking up and waiting for the first, feathery sign of white smoke which signifies, as it has for

Palazzo Venezia   Theater of Marcellus

centuries, that a new Pope has been chosen. Black smoke, created by
adding a little straw to the burning paper, means a vote, but no elec-
tion. During the Conclave of Cardinals which elected John XXIII,
somebody forgot to put on the straw after the first ballot, and a half
million people cheered wildly for some minutes until the straw was
added and slowly the smoke turned from white to black. The Sistine
Chapel contains what doubtless must be the single most important
little stove and chimney flue in the world.

Every year hundreds of thousands of visitors come to Rome. Few
leave without seeing the Sistine Chapel. It is not an enormous room,
and for almost the whole day every day it is as crowded as Grand
Central on a holiday. Furthermore, it is clamorous with the sound
of guides explaining in half a dozen languages the meaning and sig-
nificance of the paintings. The Vatican doors are opened promptly at
9:00 A.M. If you are there in time to get one of the first ten tickets, if
you trot up the beautiful double spiral staircase just inside the entrance and without looking to right or left go as quickly as you can
without running to the Sistine Chapel—then, if you are lucky, you
may have as much as fifteen or twenty minutes of complete solitude
in this most magnificent of all rooms. The experience is overwhelming beyond description. Without much doubt it will be the most
memorable quarter of an hour of your whole trip.

Probably next in order of importance to the Vatican Museum is
the CAPITOLINE MUSEUM, actually two museums (one ticket for both),
the **Capitoline** and the **Palazzo dei Conservatori**, flanking the Piazza
del Campidoglio, which Michelangelo designed. Both have examples
of classical sculpture, and the Palazzo also has a picture gallery and
an interesting collection of objects from classical times, including a
neat and swift-looking little Roman chariot and a wooden litter to be
borne by slaves which doesn't look as comfortable as a Roman litter
ought to. The most impressive sculpture is in the Capitoline. Some of
the most celebrated pieces from antiquity are there including the
Dying Gaul, Cupid and Psyche, the *Faun* (Hawthorne's *Marble Faun*)
and, with a room all to herself, the nude and voluptuous *Capitoline
Venus.* There are innumerable portrait busts of emperors, statesmen,
and generals, all with such amazingly modern appearance that you
would not be in the least surprised to see these faces on the streets

Opera performance at the Baths of Caracalla

outside. In the Capitoline, ancient Rome becomes a very real place, and its people, even the impossible Nero and Caligula, who are represented here, alarmingly real. The *Room of the Doves* is memorable for the two perfect mosaics, one of the doves drinking from a basin, the other of the masks of comedy and tragedy, both taken from Hadrian's Villa. (Piece by piece and museum by museum you will be able to begin to appreciate some of the glories of that ruined Villa.)

Across the way, at the **Palazzo Dei Conservatori**, you pass through a courtyard with the largest stone head and the largest stone foot you're likely to see—the faces of Mt. Rushmore dutifully excepted. Both head and foot are supposed to be fragments of a statue of Constantine; they are likely to remind you of Shelley's "Ozymandius." Among the many fine pieces of sculpture inside are two which you are certain to remember: the *Boy With a Thorn,* a graceful Greek piece of a young boy pulling a thorn out of his foot, and the *She-wolf of the Capitol,* an Etruscan study of Romulus and Remus being suckled by the mythical wolf of Rome. The *Picture Gallery* is small, but selective, with a good deal of anonymous early Christian work and paintings by such masters as Veronese, Bellini, Titian, Tintoretto, Rubens, Van Dyck, Velasquez, Guido Reni, Zucchero, and Caravaggio. The famous Caravaggio *St. John the Baptist,* which seems to have nothing whatever to do with John the Baptist but is a superb study of a young man, is displayed in solitary splendor by itself.

A wonderfully selective display of classical sculpture is to be found in the **Museo Nazionale Romano,** located in the Baths of Diocletian, directly across from the railroad station. You can become distracted by the immensity of the ruined Baths and lose your way; just keep following the little signs that say *Museo.* Sculptors advise going first and without delay to the *Hall of Masterpieces,* Room V, where a handful of the finest works are displayed in a way that should please any sculptor, ancient or modern. Among these are two versions of the *Discus Thrower,* a bronze *Boxer* of amazing power and realism, and the delicate Greek *Venus of Cyrene.* After your initiation in the Hall of Masterpieces, the sculptors say, you're ready to tackle the multiplicity of the rest of the collection, secure in your own good taste and able to ignore much that doesn't interest you without a qualm.

To complete his view of ancient sculpture and art, the visitor can go to the **Museo Barracco** in the *Piccola Farnesina,* located on the south side of the Piazza San Pantaleo. This is a new museum (1948) and houses a small, but well-chosen, collection of Sumerian, Egyptian, Babylonian, Assyrian, and Phoenician art, as well as many examples of Greek and Hellenistic sculpture.

For paintings in Rome we go to the great private collections which have now been opened to the public, the remains of patrician investment in the solid capital of art. Though it is not the most extensive collection, the Galleria Borghese in the heart of the Borghese Gardens remains the most selective collection of paintings in the city. Actually the ground floor of the museum is devoted to sculpture, much of it ancient, but some, like the celebrated half-nude portrait of Pauline Borghese, more recent. Bernini's sculpture completely dominates the collection. Five pieces testify to his amazing and patient virtuosity—*David, Apollo and Daphne, The Rape of Proserpine, Aeneas and Anchises,* and the late work *Truth,* a curiously realistic and not-so-young-and-lovely female nude. On the second floor the painting gallery begins. Spaced out over nine rooms, it is not overcrowded, but reads like an almanac of great names—Andrea del Sarto, Raphael, Correggio, Perugino, Pinturicchio, Bronzino, Rubens (*The Descent From the Cross* and *Susanna and the Elders*), Titian, Veronese, El Greco, and Caravaggio. One room (Room XIV) has six paintings by Caravaggio, so hung that they may be moved to get the best light. Among these are the powerful *David With the Head of Goliath* (the head is said to be a self-portrait of Caravaggio) and the austere *St. Jerome.*

The **Galleria Colonna**, in the Palazzo Colonna, is at once an enormous private collection of paintings and an intimate view of the good life of the Roman aristocracy of the 17th, 18th, and early 19th centuries. The rooms of the gallery are not only space for the display of works of art, but are also superbly decorated and furnished as rooms. There is an amusing testimony to the effect of history on the place. On the marble stairway at the upper end of the *Great Hall* a cannonball rests, as if displayed in a place of honor, exactly where it fell during the siege of 1848. The collection is not as selective as that of the Borghese, but it is wider, covering a greater range of styles and time; and many of the masters are well represented—Bronzino, Bassano, Botticelli, Breughel, Tintoretto, Van Dyck, Veronese, and Rubens (*Reconciliation of Esau and Jacob*). In the *Room of the Desks* are a number of paintings by Claude and Poussin, two artists of special interest because they had a profound effect on American landscape painting and on American writing as well, largely through the agency of such travelers as Hawthorne and Melville, who saw their works here. (Open only on Saturday, 9 to 1.)

Night view of the Colosseum

SITES AND SITUATIONS

Rome is certainly a city of churches and museums, but it is even more a city of *places,* sites and vistas, often beautiful in themselves and always enmeshed in the rich texture of historical association. These places are unique and yet related to each other and to the whole of the city, like an archipelago of separate islands. You can begin almost anywhere, but before long your curiosity will lead you all through the city and in a circle, back to where you started.

Ancient Rome is everywhere evident—shards and fragments in the walls of later buildings, columns in the churches, triumphal arches, lonely and proud, and here and there brick foundations of what were once palaces, temples, or baths. But some ancient and splendid buildings are standing still, many of them in sufficiently good repair to give a very fair idea of what they once were.

Much of what has been preserved in its original form is within easy striking distance of the **Colosseum**. Standing huge in a great expanse of space, a landmark for the southern part of the city, it is, at first glance and by plain daylight, something of a disappointment. For it looks exactly like what it was—a huge public stadium. Since so many of our own big stadiums have been built with it as a model, we tend by a curious process of inverse historical thinking to overlook its novelty and immensity. When you enter the great circular walls, you are due for other disappointments. Excavations have peeled back the earth inside the oval to reveal the foundations and the subterranean passages and quarters. You may well be surprised that the space inside seems small and cluttered. And every guide, official or unofficial, will be quick to tell you that Nero never saw the place and that it's probable that no Christians ever died there. To which you can't reply —except, perhaps, to say that human history is more than facts. History is just as much what we choose to believe about our past. And the plain, consecrated cross in the Colosseum is not an irónic mistake, but an aptly placed memorial for the Christians who died, elsewhere, it may be, under Roman persecution.

By day it is best to ignore the ground level with its loafers and loungers, its guides and tourists, its souvenir and soft drink stands.

(Though, if you happen to be thirsty, the Italian soft drinks, particularly the orangeade, *aranciata,* and lemonade, *limonata,* made from fresh fruit and local mineral waters instead of carbonated water, are eminently satisfying.) Climb by the stairway on the north side (you pay a fee about halfway up) to the top gallery. There you will get a better conception of the real size and scope of the place. You will also have a fine vantage point from which to view the city. Come by night, preferably with at least a little moonlight, to look at the ground level after the crowds have gone home, and silence has settled over the place. The Colosseum then becomes a thing of shadows where ghosts stir and set your imagination to dancing.

Between the Colosseum and the river is the **Palatine Hill**. Here, where Rome began, it has now almost returned to nature. It is like a large park with, here and there, the fragmentary ruins of the imperial palaces. There is a section of well-laid-out garden, the *Farnese Gardens,* dating from the 16th century; a Palatine Museum and a couple of outbuildings with archeological finds; and the *Palatine Antiquariam,* occupying the site of a former convent. Many important buildings once stood on this hill—houses for the great, like Domitian's Palace, lavish beyond believing. It must have been crowded then. But unless you are an archeologist or more skilled than most of us at reconstructing buildings in imagination from the evidence of a few brick foundations, you are likely to remember the Palatine Hill as a quiet green place in the midst of the city, a place with paths and flowers and vistas in all directions.

Closer to the river and not far from the Piazza Venezia are the remains of the **Theater of Marcellus**. Begun by Julius Caesar and finished by Augustus, it was large enough to hold twenty thousand imperial spectators. It has had a long and varied history, and like so many remains of ancient Rome, its story has not yet ended. After the fall of Rome it was used as a quarry for a time. In the 12th century it

Ancient ruins on the Palatine Hill

was made into a fortress, and in the 16th transformed from fortress to palace, always, of course, retaining its basic shape and form unchanged. Now it is an apartment house. You will see diapers flapping on wash lines strung across the high galleries.

A little to the south, near the river, and facing the Piazza della Bocca della Verità, are two well-preserved (and restored) temples which will give you a better idea of what a Roman temple actually was than any number of large ruins. The **Temple of Fortuna Virilis**, an excellent example of a structure from the days of the Roman Republic, was preserved largely because it became a church during the Middle Ages. Near it is the small, circular **Temple of Vesta**.It, too, did duty as a church and thus was saved for our times.

The most perfectly preserved of all ancient Roman structures— and next to the Colosseum, the most famous—is the **Pantheon**. It is made of brick and covered with a huge concrete dome. The exterior of the Pantheon remains much as it always was. The interior, however, was thoroughly looted of its marble, its bronze statues (for Bernini's Baldachino at St. Peter's), its precious coffering and ornaments. The interior is lighted only through an opening in the center of the dome, a twenty-eight-foot open circle a hundred feet above the floor. Rain pours through the large hole and spatters on the *pavimento* below. In this building the kings of Italy, beginning with Victor Emmanuel II in 1878, are buried, and here too lies Raphael, surrounded now by royalty and dignitaries of state.

Across the Tiber, just at the end of the ancient (and narrow) Ponte S. Angelo, stands the massive and formidable **Castel S. Angelo**. It was originally a tomb, the *Mausoleum of Hadrian,* and until the time of Caracalla, the Roman emperors and their families were buried there. In the Middle Ages it was transformed into what it now is, a Papal fort. From the Vatican gardens an escape route known as the "covered way" still leads to the castle. It was used more than once in the past, and tradition still requires that a Swiss guard stand at the Vatican door to the route, with the key in his possession at all times. The castle now houses a museum, the *Museo Nazionale di Castel S. Angelo,* which, among other exhibits, contains one of the best collections of warlike gear in the world, from the Stone Age to the present. There are works of art, too, and luxurious Papal apartments, but the fortress (which for a time was also a prison) remains unchangingly grim and dark.

Not much, really, is left of the **Forum** except the space where it once stood. Most impressive of the remaining structures are the *Arch of Septimius Severus* at the end of the Forum towards the Capitoline Hill, the six perfect columns and the pediment of *The Temple to Antoninus and Faustina,* and the three stark, fluted columns, over forty feet high, that mark the place of the beautiful *Temple of Castor and Pollux.* The rest of the area looks at first like nothing so much as a rock-strewn field. But once you've entered the precincts and gone

The Pantheon—one of the world's great architectural achievements

down on the field you discover that the celebrated *Sacra Via,* the paved road that led through the Forum, is still there. It is enchanted ground after all. Everyone in ancient Rome walked on these very stones, you suddenly remember, at some time. The Forum, which is still being painstakingly excavated, has been so thoroughly studied by scholars that with the official handbook and map you can find the remains of every walk and building you've ever read about—the *Temple of Julius Caesar,* the *Curia,* the *Lapis Niger* (a pavement of black marble laid on a sacred place), the *Rostra,* the *Temple of Saturn, Basilica Julia, House and Temple of the Vestals,* and many others. In at least this one fabulously rich area, the science of archeology has distinguished itself. Every stone is a definite clue in this huge historical jigsaw puzzle, and every column speaks of the glory of Rome at its height.

Between the Colosseum and the Piazza Venezia runs the wide modern avenue, the Via dei Fori Imperiali. On either side of it are a succession of ruins from all periods of ancient Rome. At the Venezia end, just across from the Victor Emmanuel Monument, is the **Forum of Trajan,** where stands the single, intricately carved *Trajan Column.* Nearby are patches and remnants of other forums—the **Forum of Julius Caesar,** of **Augustus,** and of **Nerva.** Beneath the Via dei Fori Imperiali itself lies the still buried **Forum of Vespasian.**

No listing of the Roman ruins in the center of town would be complete without mentioning the **Baths of Diocletian** and the **Baths of Caracalla.** Both are ruins, huge brick remnants of what they once were. And they must have been something once. The thought of the lavish Roman baths, with their hot rooms and cold, games, and massages, is intriguing to us in the time of the one-man tub. The Baths of Diocletian, of course, have now become a church and a good museum. The Baths of Caracalla, more scenic and, in parts, better preserved, provide a handsome setting for summer opera and ballet under the stars. The performances are so well mounted and pleasurable that you will surely thank the ancient Romans for their curious habit of bathing en masse.

If you drive south from the center of the city by car or bus, you find yourself suddenly out of the flow of traffic and riding along on a road called the **Via Appia Antica** which the Romans built in 312 B.C. (Many of the Roman paving stones remain.) Far off, paralleling the road, are the ruins of a great aqueduct. You pass by the *Tomb of the Scipios,* the *Arch of Drusus,* the *Porta San Sebastiano,* with its twin crenelated towers, and come to the area of the **Catacombs**. There are other catacombs in Rome proper, and some are found even on the other side of the Janiculum and beyond the Porta San Pancrazio. But those along the Appian Way are the most famous. In these labyrinthine passages the early Christians buried their dead, hid during periods of persecution, and held their forbidden services. Some sections of these dank and eerie tunnels can be visited. Not so very long ago, each visitor was given a candle to light his way through the darkness. Today, the passages are lighted (occasionally) by bare light bulbs. But it is still advisable to stick close to your group and your guide. It would not be difficult to get lost in this maze of tunnels; to find your way out would be another matter altogether. The principal catacombs, entered through churches on the spot or nearby, are the *Catacombs of Calixtus,* of *St. Cecilia,* of *Domitilla,* and of *St. Sebastian.* Within there is much to be seen besides the bones of long departed Christians—chapels, including the *Chapel of the Popes* in Calixtus, strange and intriguing inscriptions, and ancient decorations.

The Appian Way once was lined with Roman tombs and monuments as far from Rome as Albano. Most of them were destroyed long ago. The **Tomb of Cecilia Metella**, just beyond the Catacombs, is one well-preserved example, and further along there are the ruins of other stately monuments. In very recent times the Appian Way has become fashionable for the living.

Many modern villas have sprung up nearby, and the Appian Way is rapidly becoming a popular residential area, particularly for such newly rich as the movie people.

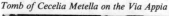
Tomb of Cecelia Metella on the Via Appia

PIAZZAS AND PLACES

Sooner or later every American who comes to Rome goes to the **Piazza di Spagna**. One reason is that American Express has its office there, but it is also a justly popular spot in its own right. It is a small piazza which, mercifully, has recently been blocked from traffic, and the little boat-fountain, the *Barcaccia*, designed by Pietro Bernini, now stands peacefully in the center. Across from the fountain are the much-celebrated and altogether beautiful *Spanish Steps*. They lead up in a series of graceful flights to the twin spires of the church of *Trinità dei Monti*. There are flower markets under colorful umbrellas at the foot of the Spanish Steps, and in the spring for a brief while the whole stairway is banked with the white and red of potted azaleas.

Next to the steps is the *Keats-Shelley Memorial,* in a house containing the apartment where John Keats died. It is something no English-speaking visitor should miss, a well-kept museum and one of the finest collections of the Romantic poets, and books pertaining to them and their work in the world. Every year eminent American and British scholars come to Rome to work in that library. Every visiting author shows up; the guest book reads like a literary Who's Who. The custodian for many years (more than thirty) has been an Italian lady who speaks perfect English and lives in the apartment directly above the one where Keats lived. She is Vera Cacciatore, a distinguished Italian novelist. Her husband, the poet Eduardo Cacciatore, often does his writing where Keats himself worked, on the little balcony in back, overlooking the Spanish Steps.

Not far away and, like the Spanish Steps area, on the fringe of what the Italians call "Little America," is the *Piazza Barberini*. Out of it flows the chic Via Veneto, where the American Embassy and many fashionable hotels and sidewalk cafés are located. (Also nearby on the Via Veneto is the USIS Library, where you can see the latest publications from home.) The Piazza is renowned for the fountain by Bernini—the *Fontana del Tritone*—a Baroque piece built around four dolphins supporting a large shell on which sits a Triton blowing a stream of water from a conch shell.

At the edge of the piazza next to the Via Veneto is a Capuchin convent and its church of *S. Maria della Concezione.* This church is noted for its cemetery (above ground), consisting of four chambers elaborately decorated with the bones and mummified bodies and skulls of monks who died there. Hawthorne and Hans Christian Andersen were horrified. Many modern visitors are too.

In a magnificent location just beneath the Pincian Hill, overhung by the green profusion of the Borghese Gardens, is the **Piazza del Popolo**, part of a trinity or triangle of great piazzas. The *obelisk* in the center is the largest, and the second oldest object in Rome. Nero is said to be buried to the left of the piazza near the church of S. Maria del Popolo.

The Spanish Steps and San Trinità Dei Monti

The inevitable piazza, the one that you have to pass through many times during your stay in Rome, is the **Piazza di Venezia**. This huge square with important thoroughfares entering it from six directions is usually regarded as the true center of the modern city. Certainly Mussolini thought of it in this way, for the small balcony from which he ruled a brief empire and addressed the crowds is easily seen along the otherwise plain façade of the *Palazzo Venezia,* along the west side of the square. When he stood on that perch, he could look to the left and see the Corso running all the way across town to the obelisk of the Piazza del Popolo. Straight ahead he could see the beginning of the spacious Via dei Fori Imperiali, which he himself built, running to the Colosseum. To his right towered the dazzling white marble of the *Monument of Victor Emmanuel II.* This most familiar of modern Roman landmarks, the grave of Italy's Unknown Soldier, is guarded day and night by sentries. It also houses the *Museo del Risorgimento,* dedicated to the long struggle for the unification of Italy in the 19th century.

Directly across the piazza from the Monument is the entrance to the **Corso**, probably Rome's busiest street. At the entrance, surrounded on all sides by raging traffic, stands a single policeman on a raised circular platform running the whole show in the piazza by hand. His is perhaps the least enviable job in Rome, so tough that the man who draws the assignment is relieved after half an hour. But while he is there, the exhibition of his white-gloved skill is something to behold.

Almost equally busy is the **Piazza della Repubblica** (formerly, and still often, called the Piazza dell' Esedra), a large graceful circle at the end of the Via Nazionale. The Baths of Diocletian face on this piazza, and the railroad station is nearby. Besides its important central location, the piazza is noted for its modern fountain, *The Fountain of the Naiads* (1901), one of the largest in Rome. Because it stands on high ground, the great main jet can be seen playing from almost half a mile away at the foot of the Via Nazionale. At night it is skillfully illuminated.

The fountain is an integral part of the whole experience of a piazza. No piazza in all of Rome better illustrates this than the **Piazza Navona**. From any direction you enter by dark, ancient streets. You first hear the sound of falling water, and then quite suddenly you are faced with a bright, exuberant explosion of open space. The site is ideal. It was once the Stadium of Domitian, which, judging by the closed oval shape, is believed to have been a track for horse and chariot racing. Festivals and sports events were often held here through the centuries. Eighteenth-century prints show the piazza flooded with water, and on hot summer evenings the aristocrats drove round and round the piazza in carriages cooling themselves and splashing water on crowds of curious commoners. Nowadays when an open market and fair occupies the square from Christmas through *Befana* (Epiphany), much of the old excitement returns.

But it was Bernini who managed to make the space of the piazza the thing of beauty that it is today. Within its oval shape, two fountains at each end guard the great *Fontana dei Quattro Fiumi* (Fountain of the Four Rivers) in the center. For this fountain he created a mass of rock work and grottoes supporting a large obelisk. At the corners of the structure are four enormous figures representing the Danube, Ganges, Nile, and Plata rivers. It is an extravagant conception in water and stone, for the rock formations are so handled as to seem as fluid as water, as if water and rock were flowing together from the same source. The obelisk seems light as air, for at no point did Bernini show the points of stress where its weight is supported. At these key points the eye is fooled by the sheer activity of flowing water and the elaborate decoration of the stones. The obelisk seems to stand entirely unsupported, like a rocket just beginning its ascent into outer space. Bernini, always a playful creator, has the figure representing the Nile hiding his eyes, apparently, as the story goes, so that he won't have to look across at the façade of *S. Agnese in Agone,* a church designed by Bernini's rival, Borromini.

The Piazza Navona is a fine restful spot for footsore and weary sight-seers, an excellent place just to sit and look. There are many excellent sidewalk cafés around it for just this purpose, and one of them, the *Tre Scalini,* has some of the best and most elaborate ice cream concoctions in Rome.

One fountain dear to the hearts of all tourists and especially to Americans is the **Fontana di Trevi** in the tiny *Piazza di Trevi.* It is an enormous wall fountain made up of allegorical figures, rocks and grottoes, built, as many of the Roman fountains are, to honor a particular source of the city's varied water supply. (In this case the water is "Acqua Vergine.") It is a genuine cascade, so large that the noise is nearly deafening. More than seventeen million gallons of water a day fall from the fountain. A tradition has grown up, apparently beginning in the 19th century, that the traveler who throws a coin into the pool will surely return to Rome. So many people like to believe the legend that the pool continually glitters with coins, even though almost nightly the street urchins pick it clean.

There are a number of large parks in Rome that help to give the city its sense of green. The largest of these is the **Borghese Gardens** on the Pincian Hill. There are bridle paths (cheap, with gentle nags to ride), a Punch and Judy show, donkey carts for the children, one of the finest zoos in the world (where, by a trick and careful landscaping, wild animals seem to be on the loose), and splendid vistas of the city. The **Janiculum** offers a smaller park and a wider, higher view of the whole town from the other side of the Tiber. Not far from the park of the Janiculum is the **Villa Sciarra**, once the grounds of a rich private villa, now a beautifully laid out park, with antique statues, flowers, peacocks, fountains, a little carousel run by hand and, of course, the inevitable donkey carts. Popular with the Romans, especially the children, the Villa Sciarra is seldom visited by tourists. It's worth seeing if only because it gives you the best chance you will ever have to see what the grounds of the great villas and palaces were actually like. Those that have been opened to the public are not as well kept as this one; those that are still private you will never see.

Perhaps the most charming park, and certainly the most amusing view of the city, is behind a locked gate that you are not likely ever to enter. This gate faces on the **Piazza dei Cavalieri di Malta** and is the entrance to the extra-territorial Priory of the Knights of Malta with its gardens, living quarters, and chapel for the order. The piazza and all of the buildings were designed by the famous 18th-century Roman painter and engraver, Piranesi. He had a spirit as playful as that of the earlier Bernini. Knowing that the order was (and is) an exclusive one, and that most people would never see the work he had done behind the wall, he apparently designed the whole garden with that disturbing thought in mind. In the gate he put a large keyhole. If you look through the keyhole, you see a long avenue of trees and flowers leading to a single framed vision of . . . But it's best not to say. See for yourself. It's well worth going up to the top of the quiet Aventine just to bend down and squint through a keyhole.

II: A CLOSER LOOK

In Rome you are faced with a continual problem: to see or not to see. And, having seen something once, or having seen some things especially appealing among the many, you have to decide whether to go on in search of new experiences or to return to familiar and pleasant ones. Most Romans and long-time foreign residents advise a compromise. You should go ahead—as long as you have the time—trying to see more new things, but not entirely at the expense of the old ones. Because of the peculiar unity of Rome, it is almost always possible to combine a venture into new and unexplored territory with a return visit to the familiar. That kind of compromise is thoroughly in keeping with the spirit of Rome, and it is with that in mind that this second look at the city has been written.

PLACES AND BUILDINGS

As you must have discovered by this time, a good place to begin anything in Rome is with a fountain, and a good place to begin a closer look at the city is with one of the smaller, less-known fountains, for example the simple and charming *Fontana delle Tartarughe* (Tortoise Fountain) in the tiny **Piazza Mattei**.

Here you find yourself in the heart of medieval Rome, at the edge of the old *Ghetto,* but scarcely a stone's throw away from one of the busy centers of traffic and a main bus terminal for the city's bus lines —the *Largo Argentina.* This square is of interest chiefly for its large centerpiece, the fenced-in ruins of the *Four Republican Temples,* which are interesting and impressive in themselves. But you are likely to remember this as the place you saw the fabled cats of Rome at close range. They wander everywhere among the ruins, wild, proud, apparently numberless and always hungry.

The Piazza Mattei with its little fountain of four tortoises stands under the shadow of three of the great Renaissance palaces of Rome: the *Palazzo Antici-Mattei,* the *Palazzo Caetani,* and the *Palazzo Costaguti.* The Costaguti palace is celebrated for its six splendid ceilings painted by great artists. The Caetani Palace, owned by one of the oldest noble families in Rome, is a still very much lived-in palace, occupied by family descendants. The Palazzo Caetani was also the home of the important modern international literary magazine *Botteghe Oscure* during its more than ten years of publication under the editorship of the Princess Caetani. The Palazzo Antici-Mattei is now owned and occupied by the *Italo-American Association.* Concerts, exhibitions, lectures, and seminars are regularly held in its splendid rooms and halls, and the library, open on weekdays, has an enviable collection of the latest American books and magazines.

The visitor who has developed a taste for old Renaissance palaces and the beauty of their courtyards will be interested in the building at Via Montserrato 20. What was once an elegant palazzo is now an apartment house. The courtyard with a garden and a good classical fountain is always open by day, and the stairway just inside is worth a climb, for the walls are studded with fascinating shards and bits of classical sculpture.

Between the Piazza Mattei and the Tiber are the twisting streets and huddled medieval buildings of the old **Ghetto**. For centuries Rome's Jewish population was forced to live there and was locked in at night. It is difficult to believe the sufferings and persecutions to which the Jews of Rome were subjected during the Middle Ages and the Renaissance. Every year during the *Carnevale* season (Mardi Gras) they were rounded up and made to run races down the whole length of the Corso, naked except for loin cloths. At the edge of the Ghetto facing the river is the small church of *S. Angelo in Pescheria* with a painting of the Crucifixion decorating the façade. Here for hundreds of years the Jews were driven every Sunday and made to listen to a sermon. Down to modern times many of Rome's Jewish families have continued to live in this section, and, needless to say, the area suffered terribly during the Nazi occupation in 1944. Now, however, it is a lively, cheerful place, shrill with the voices of playing children, a picturesque relic of the Middle Ages and graced with some of the finest eating places in the city, tucked out of sight of the casual visitor and preserved by the Romans for themselves.

Near S. Angelo in Pescheria and back to back with the Theater of Marcellus is the *Porticus of Octavia*. Only the façade and a few marble shafts remain of this structure, which was once composed of more than three hundred columns.

Looming over the whole area is the huge, gloomy *Palazzo Cenci,* long-time residence of the Cenci family and the scene of many of the bizarre crimes which stained the family name during the days of the Renaissance: murder, rape, incest, sodomy, sadistic tortures, and plain robbery. It looks fierce enough to have fostered such crimes, and mysterious enough to be guarding other black secrets as well.

Directly across from this section, reached by the oldest bridge in Rome, the *Ponte Fabricio,* is the island called **Isola Tiberina**. Since the shape of the island is rather like a ship, the Romans improved on nature by creating a pointed stone bow to breast the currents of the Tiber and by erecting a tall obelisk to represent a mast. On this small island is the 10th-century church of *S. Bartolomeo,* with a fine Romanesque tower and, inside, fourteen ancient columns. There is also a large hospital on the island, aptly so, for this was once the site of the *Temple of Aesculapius,* the Roman god of healing. His symbolic serpent is carved into the bow of the "ship."

Another fountain, and a good one, can be the occasion for a visit to an area of much interest. This fountain is a creation using two groups of the *Dioscuri* (Castor and Pollux), standing beside their mythical horses, topped by a large obelisk. The statues are Roman copies of

Greek originals which dated from the 5th century B.C. This fountain, situated in the center of the spacious **Piazza del Quirinale,** is splendidly illuminated by night. Facing the piazza are the *Palazzo della Consulta*, home of the Supreme Court, and the *Palazzo del Quirinale,* official residence of the President of the Republic. The Quirinal Palace was once the summer palace of the Popes, and many great artists, including Bernini and Maderna, had a part in enriching its decoration. In this piazza in front of the gate to the Quirinal Palace, the daily changing of the guard takes place, a festive occasion that recalls the pleasures of comic opera.

Quite near, built on the site of the *Baths of Constantine,* is the **Palazzo Rospigliosi**, considered to be one of the most attractive of the princely palaces of Rome. Its private gallery, the *Galleries Palavicini,* contains paintings by Botticelli, Rubens, Signorelli, Van Dyck, Poussin, Caravaggio, and many others. In the adjoining **Casino Rospigliosi** is the much celebrated *Fresco of Aurora* by Guido Reni. This ancient family has ties with America, and, in fact, the present Princess Rospigliosi was, for many years, Secretary to the American Academy in Rome.

Beyond the piazza, going along the **Via del Quirinale**, there are two excellent examples of Baroque art and architecture at its best: *S. Andrea al Quirinale,* a small and elegant church contrived by Bernini, and *S. Carlino,* by his rival Borromini. Just beyond the churches is an intersection called *Quattro Fontane* with four fountains, one on each corner. It is somehow typical of things Roman that all four streets coming together here offer memorable vistas.

The combination of extraordinary fountain and extraordinary vista is rare, though, even in Rome, but this happy combination is achieved on the **Janiculum**, just below the park and directly behind the Spanish Embassy, in the *Fontana Paola.* The water for this fountain comes from the subterranean Aqueduct of Trajan and spills forth from an unusual structure designed by Fontana and Maderna (of the St. Peter's piazza fountains) from some fragments of the Temple of Minerva. It is at once a splendid and curiously amusing fountain, looking rather like a triumphal arch or perhaps a classical

San Giorgio in Velabro; San Maria in Cosmedin

façade with openings, like doors and windows, out of which the water flows in cascades. The result is to make the modern viewer think of a house whose owners have gone away and left the water running. From the balustrade at the foot of the fountain there is another wonderful view of the whole city.

A block down the hill is the church of *S. Pietro in Montorio,* where, tradition has it, Beatrice Cenci is buried. The interior has celebrated frescoes by Vasari and a chapel designed by Bernini. The cloister has the famous domed *Tempietto* of Bramante mentioned earlier.

Above the fountain, bordering on the park of the Janiculum, is the *American Academy,* where American scholars, painters, sculptors, musicians, composers, and writers come to live and work. It is housed in a Roman-style palazzo built by the venerable and historic American architectural firm of McKim, Meade, and White. It blends perfectly with its surroundings. Worth seeing is the courtyard, which has a single antique fountain in the center continually playing and walls lined with shards and fragments from many important excavations in which American archaeologists took part. There is a small and excellent museum of antiquities and a large library, open daily, which has the best collection of books on Rome in English available anywhere. And there is always the chance that the American visitor may find himself invited to see the studio of a working painter or sculptor. Exhibitions, concerts, readings, and lectures take place frequently.

Across the street from the Academy is the *Villa Aurelia,* an imposing Renaissance structure with fine gardens. It was Garibaldi's headquarters during the siege of Rome by the French. Now it belongs to the American Academy, whose director lives there.

The *Porta S. Pancrazio* stands on the summit of the Janiculum This Renaissance gate was built on the site of the ancient *Porta Aurelia,* which was (and is) the beginning of the old Roman road Via Aurelia. It was through this gate that Garibaldi's men charged to their death assaulting the *Villa Doria Pamphili,* a few hundred yards away. This villa, five and a half miles around, has been bought by the city of Rome and is now a public park.

Though it may seem redundant to the visitor who just happens to be staying in a hotel or *pensione* in the vicinity, the **Via Vittorio Veneto**, from the *Piazza Barberini* to the *Porta Pia* presents a special aspect of modern Rome that shouldn't be missed. This modern street —once chic and elegant—now looks to some like neon village. But the *paparazzi,* Rome's scandal-hunting photographers can still be found here, and the Café de Paris, the bar that was for so long the site of "La Dolce Vita," is still there. You might get a glimpse of a film star at one of the sidewalk cafés—but don't count on it. But there are Americans aplenty as well as young Romans of every description. The Via Veneto is not what it has been. But it's still well worth spending an hour or so of an afternoon at a café to see the passing parade.

MUSEUMS AND MONUMENTS

There are all kinds and descriptions of museums in Rome. With such an embarrassment of riches in art and history, it doesn't take much effort on the part of Romans to collect enough to have a museum of some importance, by American standards, at least. Many of these smaller places are unlisted as museums, and you will discover them only as parts of churches and palaces that you visit. There are enough "official" museums in the city to keep you very busy the whole time, but there are also many lesser ones worthy of attention by any standard.

One of these is the **Museo di Roma** in the Palazzo Braschi. To this museum were moved the contents of the old Museo dell'Impero Romano in the Piazza della Bocca Verita. The Museo di Roma now includes in its important modern section a representative collection of paintings, drawings, and prints illustrating the life and history of Rome from medieval times to the present. If you have acquired a favorite vista or site in Rome, it may be of interest to see how much or how little it has changed over the years. There is also a *Gallery of Modern Art* in the museum, one of two such public galleries in Rome.

For the very latest in modern art, including the work of many American artists who are living in Rome, the **Marlborough Gallery,** Via Gregoriana 5, is among the best known of the commercial galleries. In the **Via Margutta,** an artists' quarter a few blocks from the Spanish Steps, are various other small galleries.

The other, and the most important gallery of modern art in Rome, the **Galleria Nazionale d'Arte Moderna,** is in the Palazzo delle Belle Arti near the zoo in the Borghese Gardens. This gallery contains a large and extensive collection of Italian painting and sculpture from the 18th century to the present time, and in addition there is usually an exhibition of some importance being shown there. And with lots of space at their disposal, they usually display things in an enviable manner.

In the field of painting there remains one important gallery which is often overlooked, the **Galleria Spada** in the Palazzo Spada. A small, personal collection, it was begun by Cardinal Bernadino Spada and continued by his family. It specializes in 17th- and 18th-century painting and, in addition, displays some ancient sculpture.

The **Accademia di San Luca** is a fine arts academy located in the Palazzo Carpegna, begun in the 16th century. Over the years it has amassed a considerable collection of paintings. Among the major artists represented are: Raphael, Bronzino, Titian, Van Dyck, Rubens, and Guido Reni.

Almost next door to this Academy, in the Via delle Muratte, is the **Calcografia Nazionale** with one of the world's greatest collection of copperplate engravings.

An equally specialized museum, and a most interesting one, is the **Napoleonic Museum** in the Palazzo Pumoli. This museum contains

nineteen rooms of works of art and relics which belonged to the
Bonaparte family. Napoleon briefly ruled Rome, his sister married
a Borghese prince, and his mother lived in a palace there until her
death. So the museum is of dual interest, first in terms of one of modern history's great men and, secondly, because it offers a rare record
of the city during the early years of the 19th century.

While he ruled Rome, Napoleon freely appropriated what he
wanted for France from the great collections of the city. One collection he rather systematically looted (294 pieces shipped home to
France) was that of the **Villa Albani** (also called the Villa Torlonia).
This was, and is still, one of the most famous collections of classical
sculpture, for it was the first one collected and arranged scientifically
and systematically. It was created for the Cardinal Albani by the man
who is called the father of the science of archeology—Winckelmann.
Even after Napoleon went through the collection with a fine-tooth
comb, it remained a great collection, and it has been added to since.

To see it you must file an application with the *Amministrazione Torlonia,* Via della Conciliazione 30. This requirement is less formidable
than it sounds. Other collections in the city require the same kind of
thing, and you needn't hesitate going through the motions if you're
interested. It seems to be a device intended primarily to keep out idle
sight-seers who just happen to be passing by.

The collection in the Villa Albani includes a vast array of classical
sculpture, inscriptions, and objects, among them many Etruscan remains. Of special interest is a very rare set of Etruscan wall paintings transferred from their original tombs on Albani property. There
are wide gardens and walks dotted with pieces of classical sculpture,
but the main collection is within the Villa itself. No one lives in the
building today, but the children of the noble family which owns it occasionally play in the extensive grounds. You will be delighted by the
incongruity of a collection of very modern toys kept there for them—
aircraft, tanks, cars, trucks, etc.—just inside the front door of the
Villa. In addition to sculpture and other antiquities, the Villa includes
a small painting gallery with, among others, the following well-
known artists represented: Raphael Mengs, Perugino, Van Dyck, and
Tintoretto. On the second floor is preserved, in intricate detail, the
bedchamber of the Cardinal Albani.

If very ancient things interest you, you won't want to miss the
Museo Preistorico on the Via del Collegio Romano. It is a large museum of pre-Etruscan findings in Italy, going back to Stone Age im-
plements. There are other objects from Asia and the Middle East
here as well.

You don't have to go to museums, though, to find the mark and
signature of ancient Rome. One of its permanent and, strangely,
commonplace bequests to the modern city is the ruins of the old
walls. The earliest known wall was around the settlement on the Palatine Hill, and fragments of it have been found. But the two chief

Remains of the House of the Vestals in the Roman Forum

walls of ancient Rome are still very much in evidence, and many of their gates are still used by modern traffic. The first of these is the **Servian Wall**, existing in bits and stretches, part of which, as we noted, runs into the modern railroad station, the Stazione Termini. But the great wall, and one which is largely preserved, is the **Aurelian Wall**, circling the seven hills of the city as well as the other side of the Tiber, Trastevere, and part of the Janiculum.

In addition to the walls the ancient Romans left behind them their triumphal arches, magnificent structures through which emperors and their cohorts once paraded their captives in triumph. The most familiar of these arches, because of postcard photographs and because of its location (almost within the shadow of the Colosseum) and relative isolation (that is, not attached to any other structure) is the noble **Arch of Constantine**. Actually three arches joined in one, it stands at the south end of the Piazzale del Colosseo. The Arch of Constantine is a graphic illustration that the Romans apparently have always made use of their past to create the present, for it is itself made up of the fragments of earlier triumphal arches.

The **Arch of Septimius Severus**, standing as it does at one end of the Forum, is also a familiar landmark. It is an interesting proof that powerful men of the past were not above tampering with history to suit themselves and, ironically, with about as little success as modern dictators who have tried to rewrite the past. This triumphal arch was originally raised by the Senate and the people of Rome to honor the victories of Septimius Severus and his two sons, Geta and Caracalla. Some years later Caracalla murdered his brother and had Geta's name deleted from the structure. But marble is hard to erase. The holes where the original letters were are clearly visible, and the passage of time has served to make them more obvious, in the end only emphasizing the evil in Caracalla.

Also near the Forum, standing on the Clivus Sacer just above it, is the **Arch of Titus**. It was once incorporated into a string of personal fortifications put up by the battling Frangipangi family. These accretions have been torn down, and now the arch stands alone again.

The last of the really well-preserved arches is the four-sided **Arch of Janus,** which is found on the tiny, dead-end Via del Velabro, just beside the Piazza Bocca della Verita. Like Constantine's Arch, it is made up of the useful fragments of a number of earlier triumphal arches. It adjoins the ancient and seldom-visited 6th-century church, **S. Giorgio in Velabro.**

You begin to grow accustomed to stray columns and obelisks as you move about the city. They seem so naturally and inevitably a part of the scene as to be ordinary. But one column that always catches the eye, partly because of its central location in the Piazza Colonna along the busy Corso, partly because of its size and doric simplicity, is the **Column of Marcus Aurelius**. Around this column once were important Imperial buildings. All traces of them are long gone. Like the huge Column of Trajan in the Forum of Trajan, this one is intricately carved with an ascending series of bas-reliefs celebrating the victories of the emperor whose name it bears.

There is one relic of ancient Rome which you might not notice at all since it is still being used for its original purpose. On the Via Castro Pretorio, not far from the Stazione Termini is the ancient **Castro Pretorio,** once the headquarters and barracks of the crack Roman household troops, the Praetorian Guard. This group, roughly ten thousand men, was so powerful that it made and broke emperors. The building is now the Caserma del Macao, a modern Italian military barracks.

Two major examples of modern excavation and reconstruction are to be found in the Piazza Augusto Imperatore. One, the **Mausoleum of Augustus**, was a sacred monument, a large circular structure once covered with a hill-size heap of earth on which a cypress grove was planted. A great statue of the emperor stood there, amid the cypress trees. Excavations in our times have revealed the basic rooms inside the mausoleum. Like almost everything else, it was well used after its time. It was a fortress, a quarry, an amphitheater, and has been used in recent times as a concert hall.

A neighbor of the Mausoleum is the **Ara Pacis Augustae**, a monumental Roman altar now enclosed in a simple building. The altar, consecrated in 13 B.C., had the usual fate of Roman stones to start with. It was broken up into many parts, some of which wandered as far as the Louvre. In recent times the Italian government performed a superb excavation, finding every available fragment left on the spot. Scholarship coming close to detective work located the other parts wherever they were. Then patiently, piece by piece, the parts were put back together. Those that could not be regained or moved were exactly copied. And now it is there to be seen, almost as good as new.

While the emperors built arches to celebrate their triumphs, and mausoleums to celebrate their souls, the Christians of Rome were underground in catacombs. The most famous of the catacombs are those along the Via Appia Antica, mentioned earlier. But Rome has many other catacombs for the interested visitor to see.

Within the framework of the modern city, just off the Via Flaminia are the **Catacombs of St. Valentine**. They are open daily. Next to the entrance to the catacombs are the ruins of the early **Christian Basilica of St. Valentine.**

Farther out, a mile beyond the Porta Pia, within the church of S. Agnese fuori le Mura, is the entrance to the **Catacombs of St. Agnes**. The church itself is decorated with inscriptions taken from the catacombs. Though they contain no paintings, they are considered to be the best preserved of all the ancient catacombs.

At the Piazza di Priscilla is the entrance to the **Catacombs of Priscilla**, the oldest of the catacombs. They contain many interesting Christian paintings and frescoes, among them a 2nd-century painting of the Virgin and Christ Child, the earliest known.

The Via Salaria has several noted catacombs. The **Catacombs of S. Ermete**, which were not discovered until the 19th century and are still being explored, have produced several significant paintings and frescoes. The **Catacombs of Trasone** are noted for the great depth of the tunneling, and the nearby **Catacombs of S. Felicita** reveal an ancient underground basilica.

There are other burial grounds in Rome besides the pagan Roman tombs and the Christian catacombs. It was from the Jews that the Christians adopted the idea of digging catacombs in the first place. There are elaborate networks of *Jewish catacombs* on the Via Nomentana between the Porta Pia and S. Agnese fuori le Mura. However, the largest and most interesting of the Jewish catacombs is on the Via Appia Antica, amid the Christian catacombs. Its entrance is 19a Via Appia.

Naturally there aren't any Protestant catacombs, but there is the beautiful and historic **Protestant Cemetery** in Rome. Near the Porta San Paola, it is a walled place, lush and green with its many fine cypress trees. The cemetery is divided into two parts, the *Old Cemetery* where the earliest graves date from 1738, and the *New*. In the Old Cemetery there is one grave which attracts many literary pilgrims, that of John Keats, who died in what is now the Keats-Shelley Memorial House on the Piazza di Spagna. The inscription is so often misquoted or misunderstood that it deserves to be quoted in full:

> "This grave contains all that was mortal of a young English poet, who, on his deathbed, in the bitterness of his heart at the malicious power of his enemies, desired these words to be engraven on his tombstone: 'Here lies one whose name was writ in water.' February 24th, 1821"

Near Keats' grave is the grave of his friend, Joseph Severn, the English artist who cared for him during his last illness.

In the New Cemetery is the grave of Keats' contemporary, the poet Shelley. His ashes are buried alongside those of the swash-buckling soldier of fortune and friend of poets, Edward Trelawny.

The **Pyramid of Caius Sestius,** 60 feet high, towers over the cemetery. Built in about 12 A.D., it is the only pyramid in Rome, and a landmark in this part of the city.

Near it is the **Monte Testaccio**, a high and thoroughly artificial hill. It was once the dumping ground for the terra-cotta pots and jars which had been used in shipping grain and wine to the ancient Romans. Millions of them were broken and dumped here and gradually pressed down until they formed the artificial strata of a hill. It is one of the easiest places in the city to scratch the ground and pick up a free and perfectly legal souvenir of ancient Rome.

CHURCHES

A second, closer look at the churches of Rome is, in essence, an enormously ambitious project. Romans who are obsessed with the subject have never seen all of them. Art historians who come here from all over the world to study the art and architecture of Roman churches shrug, Italian-style, at the very idea of setting out on a tour of them. But you will find that in spite of these discouraging facts, you can see a great many churches while you are in Rome and get a great deal from the experience. There are various ways to go about it. Once you are familiar with the great and famous churches you may simply want to follow the hit-or-miss method—simply going into any church building that looks interesting, and having a look around. *If* it's open, and most of them are, at least in the early morning hours and again in the late afternoon. Another method is to take an area, say Trastevere, and then to cover it. Still others suggest that you look for churches of a particular period or those which have paintings by a single artist.

The truth is that for the tourist visiting Rome briefly, almost any system will work. The main thing is—like cleaning up after a party—to get started somewhere, and the rest will follow. The point is to begin.

One of the best places to begin a closer look at Rome's churches is with the church of **S. Clemente**, at the foot of the Coelian Hill and between the Colosseum and St. John Lateran. S. Clemente, in spite of some 18th-century modernizations, retains more of the details of pristine ecclesiastical architecture than any other church in Rome. The porch, made up of Ionic columns, leads into an *atrium,* a grassy courtyard with, of course, a fountain playing and the rich green leaves and spun-sugar pink blossoms of oleanders. You enter the building and find yourself in the *Upper Church,* a pure and simple basilica divided by two rows of columns. The floor is of *comatesque* work, and there is a raised choir like the one in S. Marie in Cosmedin. Around the altar and decorating the apse of the church are excellent

Interior of the Basilica of St. John Lateran

12th-century mosaics. The side chapels are decorated with early Christian and pre-Renaissance paintings.

Here you are in the Middle Ages, but by taking a flight of stairs, adorned with many fragments including a rare statuette of St. Peter as the Good Shepherd, you enter the *Lower Church,* first discovered in 1857, and pass abruptly back through several centuries. This is a great bare room, dimly lit, but still offering along the walls and in the niches a magnificent display of early Christian frescoes. A simple ancient altar remains in the Lower Church. Still lower, reached by another short staircase, lies the third level, dating from Christianity's underground days. Here are two rooms from Imperial times, with ornamented stucco ceilings, a Christian meeting place and a very well-preserved Mithraic temple, a suitably gloomy and mysterious monument to that lost religion of dark blood rites. Beneath this level, and as yet unexcavated, are known ruins from centuries earlier, from the days of the Roman republic. S. Clemente offers the visitor an easy, four-leveled history of Rome and the Church.

So near to S. Clemente that the two visits can easily be combined in a single excursion is **Quattro Coronati**, named in honor of the first known Christian artists, painters, and sculptors, whose religious consciences forbade them to make pagan idols and icons. Their refusal cost them their lives. The fiesta of these martyred saints is held here on November 8. The church was first built here on the site of a Temple of Minerva, in 622 A.D. In addition to the celebrated cloister, already mentioned as one of the special and little-known beauties of Rome, there is the *Chapel of St. Silvester,* belonging to the guild of sculptors and masons of Rome. The chapel contains a large number of crude and wooden frescoes, illustrating the life of St. Silvester. Despised by our grandfathers, these works are now eagerly studied by modern critics and scholars for their vigor and vitality and near-modern simplicity.

Although S. Clemente can be taken as the model of the living church, growing out of its own, as well as the pagan, past, there are many other churches in Rome, some of them seldom visited, which display much the same qualities of growth and gradual transformation.

Directly across from the Forum and under the jutting eminence of the Capitoline Hill is the little church of **S. Pietro in Carcere**. This is a consecrated chapel which opens into the *Mamertine Prison,* the traditional dungeon where St. Peter was confined awaiting execution. While he was there, he managed to convert his guards and jailers, and they too had to be executed not long after. True to Roman form, the Mamertine Prison didn't begin as a jail; it was even earlier a cistern or reservoir for the Capitoline.

Another neighbor of the Forum is the little round church of **S. Teodoro**. The present church is an 8th-century structure built on ancient ruins, possibly those of the *Temple of Romulus,* for the bronze she-wolf of the Capitoline Museum was found here. The floor of S. Teodoro is paved with an unusual variety of ancient marbles.

Churches built on the sites of prisons are not rare in Rome. One of the most interesting is **S. Nicola in Carcere**. It is found on the edge of the fine Piazza Bocca della Verita. The church, as it stands now, is a 12th-century building, occupying the site of three ancient Roman temples. The columns of those temples were put to good use, some of them built right into the outside walls for support. This is one of the few churches in Rome to show so obviously, in the walls and the façade, the direct use of its predecessors' materials. The vaults beneath the church contain the massive substructures of the Roman temples. It is not known for certain whether the foundations were an actual prison from Roman times, though there are some cells which the visitor is shown, indicating that indeed it was a prison once. The only trouble is that archeologists now date the cells from the Christian era, making it a jail where they locked up *their* enemies.

Direct use of the materials of pagan temples is well illustrated in two of Rome's better-known churches—**S. Maria Sopra Minerva** and **S. Stefano Rotundo**.

The Temple of Fortuna Virilis

Spiral Staircase, Vatican; Detail of Bernini's Crucifixion, *St. Peter's*

S. Maria Sopra Minerva stands behind the Pantheon in the Piazza della Minerva. This small piazza is one of Bernini's; it was he who created the obelisk standing on the back of an elephant, which is its familiar centerpiece and trademark. The church was built on the site of a Temple of Minerva, and, as a matter of fact, the statue of Minerva in the Vatican Museum was found there. Since its beginning, the church has undergone many transformations, but as it stands now it remains one of the very few, and the most important, example of the Gothic in Rome. Most of Rome's medieval churches are in the earlier Romanesque style. The interior, which is dark except in fine weather, has much interesting religious art. There is a Giotto crucifix. Fra Angelico, whose tomb is in the church, has left a memorable *Madonna and Child.* Bernini is represented inside by the *Tomb of Cardinal Pimentel.* But the masterpiece of the church, just to the left of the high altar, is Michelangelo's *Christ Bearing the Cross.* The high altar contains the body and many relics of St. Catherine of Siena.

The church has had a long and colorful history. For many years it has been the chief center for the Dominicans in Rome. The Inquisition left its mark, for this church was once a center of its activities. In more recent times, during the days of the Papal States, the church was a favorite of Popes. The historic Procession of the White Mule used to come here from the Vatican.

S. Stefano Rotondo on the Coelian Hill is a grimmer and more unusual church. Founded and first built in 467, it is the largest round church in the world. You enter, through a cloister attributed to Michelangelo, a round room 133 feet in diameter, encircled by two rows of columns. There are many relics in the church of St. Stephen, and his fiesta is celebrated here on December 26. But the church is mainly known for its wall frescoes by Pomerance and Tempesta depicting Christian martyrdoms. These cover the walls with horrors, beginning with the crucifixion, the slaughter of the innocents, and the stoning of St. Stephen, moving around the great circle with eighty-six terrible martyrdoms from the age of Nero through the persecutions under Julian the Apostate. These paintings shock, but they were not intended merely to be shocking, for the faces of the suffering saints and martyrs are shown as transfigured. It is symbolically apt that this church is built over an old Temple of Bacchus, god of wine and Roman joy and revelry.

In the neighborhood of S. Stefano Rotondo are two very ancient churches. Though one of them, **S. Tomaso in Formis,** began its history in 235, it is now probably best known for its attached neighbor, the **Arch of Dolabella.**

The second church is the important **S. Giovanni e Paolo,** built on the site of the house of two martyrs of the time of Julian the Apostate. Recent excavations have been carried out here under the impetus and interest of the late American Cardinal Spellman. These have revealed much. The church is on two levels. The interior of the upper level is chiefly noted for its apse, one of the rare examples of Lombard work in Rome. There are 16 ancient columns from pagan buildings and the pavement is in the *cosmatesque* style. The stone on which the two saints were beheaded is displayed. Beneath the church is the house of the saints, a two-story building containing many frescoes from the 2nd and 3rd centuries. There are pagan paintings of peacocks and wild birds and, of especial interest, a Christian fresco which is the earliest known painting of a martyrdom.

The remains of another private Roman house have been found in the church of **S. Martino al Monti**, a neighbor to the great church of San Pietro in Vincoli. This small church, which dates from 500, is famous historically as the place where the decisions of the Council of Nicaea were proclaimed, and the heretical books burned. On the level below the upper church is a private chapel of the 3rd century.

A neighbor of S. Martino is **S. Prassede**, which began as an oratory in 150. The present building dates from 822 and the *campanille* from 1110. The earliest known work of Bernini is in this church, but it is best known to art lovers for its elaborate *Chapel of St. Zeno (or Orto*

Part of the ancient Servian Wall near the Station

del Paradiso), a chapel entirely lined, walls and ceiling, with glittering Byzantine mosaics. The chapel contains one of the great relics of Christendom, a fragment of the column brought back by Crusaders from Jerusalem, believed to be the column on which Christ was bound and flagellated. The church also offers mosaics and wall paintings from the 9th, 12th, and 13th centuries, and it guards many other holy relics including some pieces of the Crown of Thorns and a lock of the Virgin's hair.

Another ancient church, conveniently located next to the Piazza di Venezia, is the church of **S. Marco**. It was founded in the time of Constantine, rebuilt in 833, and finally somewhat modernized in 1744. Its portico is extremely interesting for its collection of early Christian inscriptions. The fiesta of St. Mark is held here on April 25. In the vicinity of S. Marco is the famous church, **Il Gesù**, built in the 16th century to serve as the chief church of the Jesuit order. It is one of the two examples in Rome of the elegant, so-called Jesuit style, composed of an overwhelming richness of many-colored marbles and much decoration. The other Jesuit church, a rival in opulence to Il Gesù, is **S. Ignazio** on the Via del Caravita. It is built on Roman ruins and underneath it are remains of the *Aqueduct of Acqua Virgine.*

The visitor to Rome wouldn't ordinarily think of going to Trastevere to see churches, except maybe to pay a visit to S. Maria in Trastevere. But there are important churches in that area, which should not be missed.

Best known of these is **S. Cecilia in Trastevere**. The foundations of the church date from the 3rd century, and the portico is made up of ancient Roman pillars. The *campanille* dates from the 12th century, and the interior was done over in a *rococo* style in 1599, but not so as to damage the chief beauties of the Gothic canopy over the high altar and 9th-century mosaics in the apse. There are frescoes by Pinturicchio and paintings by Guido Reni to be seen, as well as the famous statue of *St. Cecilia* by Stefano Maderno.

Especially interesting are the *chambers from the house of St. Cecilia,*

View of the Tiber and Ponte Flaminio

opening out of the right aisle. These are two rooms from an old Roman house. One of them was the bath, and it still has pipes and a large bronze cauldron for heating water. The fiesta of St. Cecilia is held here on November 22, and since this *is* Trastevere and since St. Cecilia is patron saint of music, it's a colorful and noisy celebration.

Near to S. Cecilia is the church of **S. Francesco a Ripa** (1231). It was on this site that St. Francis lived when he was is Rome, and his simple cell is preserved there. This church also contains one of Bernini's most celebrated statues—the *Blessed Luisa Albertoni*.

Between S. Cecilia and the equally famous S. Maria in Trastevere is a small but important church—**S. Crisogono.** It is an ancient church, worked on in the 8th, 12th, and 17th centuries, and bears the cumulative marks of all these periods. It has a fine medieval tower, a portico of four very old columns and a *cosmatesque* pavement. The stalls are examples of modern wood carving.

Directly across the street from the church is preserved a Roman fire station—**the Guardroom of the Seventh Cohort of Vigiles.** There you can see mosaics and paintings and devices for central heating, but most interesting are the *graffiti,* the carvings and scribblings on the walls by the firemen who were stationed here in ancient times. Except for being in Latin, which makes them rather elegaic and even a little academic today, these vows, thoughts, pure exclamations, and curses turn out to be about what you might expect to find on the walls of a modern barracks.

Two other Trastevere churches well worth seeking out and seeing are: **S. Maria dell' Orto** and **S. Benedetto.** S. Maria dell' Orto was built in 1556 as the guild church of the local spaghetti-makers, ham-curers, and fruit-growers. It contains some interesting 17th century tomb carvings.

S. Benedetto on the Piazza San Benedetto a Piscinula, is built on the site of the house St. Benedict lived in. It has the original cell of the saint as well as his stone pillow. The 13th-century brick *campanile* of the church is especially fine though not well known.

Trastevere lies directly below the Janiculum, where there is a little church within sight of the Garibaldi Monument, which deserves the attention of the visitor on two counts. **S. Onofrio** has many significant pieces of art, including two paintings by Pinturicchio, but it is chiefly known for the whole building of which it is a part—the *Ospedale del Bambino Gesù.* This was once a famous monastery, and it was here that Tasso, the great Italian poet who had come to Rome to be crowned laureate, died. In his memory they keep the *Museo Tassiano* with relics of the poet's life, his death mask, manuscripts, and works. The Ospedale (now a children's hospital) is managed by the American Friars of Atonement.

On a path in the park just across from S. Onofrio is a twisted and gnarled oak tree planted there by Tasso centuries ago. It has been struck by lightning and blasted by all kinds of wind and weather. A few years ago a green shoot suddenly appeared growing from the venerable (and presumably quite dead) relic itself. This seemed exactly, aptly Roman. It seems even more so now that the shoot on *Tasso's Oak* has continued to grow and prosper.

This discussion of the old churches of Rome completely overlooks the fact that the modern Romans are still busy building new ones. You see them all over town, and on the outskirts of the city are several strikingly modernistic churches, all steel and poured concrete and glass. There is one in particular that no visitor should miss. It is on the Aventine, so close to the famous *keyhole* that you could hit it with this book. **S. Anselmo**, amid the venerable buildings of the Aventine, couldn't be built of modern materials in a modern style. It had to fit into its distinguished location. So it was created in an excellent imitation of the Romanesque style (so good that many people think it is original) with a *campanile* and a lovely rose garden in the courtyard. But it is not for the solution of an architectural problem that S. Anselmo is distinguished. It is for music. This is the only church in all of Rome where the Gregorian Chant is kept as a regular part of the regular service. The old traditions of the chant are preserved there by the monks who sing in the choir, young men, many of whom are Americans.

It was Gibbon who, sitting on the back steps of S. Maria in Aracoeli, heard the mournful singing of the choir there and began to ponder on the decline and fall of things Roman. It led to a great book. But Gibbon never had a chance to hear a Gregorian Chant sung by the young male voices of S. Anselmo. If he had, his thoughts might have turned in another direction, away from dark speculation on the past to the most remarkable idea that Rome has to offer, that of an eternal city as old as time and yet forever young.

CHAPTER 5

More than any other city in Italy, Rome is generously supplied with the widest possible variety of hotel accommodations. That is not to say that rooms are always easily available. There are times during the busy tourist season when comfortable and attractive lodging is at a premium. But if you take the simple precaution of making reservations in good time, you will be very well housed in Rome. You can choose a busy, fashionable, de luxe hotel or a quiet, elegant one. You can put up at a brand-new hotel with air conditioning, room telephones, and all the latest gadgets, or in an old *palazzo* with high-ceilinged charm and Renaissance atmosphere. Or you can decide between a small, family-style pension or a larger, more impersonal one. Finding the right hotel in Rome is merely a matter of knowing a little about what is available and a little more about your own preferences.

CHOOSING YOUR HOTEL

Price is important, of course, but even for those traveling on a close budget it is not the only consideration. More important, perhaps, for most people, is the location of the hotel. Since Rome is large and has hotels in several different sections, each with its own distinctive characteristics, you should decide first in which area you want to stay. After that it is easy enough to select a hotel that is right for you. Here, then, is a little background to help you choose a neighborhood.

The most fashionable hotels are in the Via Veneto-Piazza Barberini-Trinità dei Monti section. If you think you would like to stay on the Via Veneto and enjoy its outdoor cafés, you will find many hotels of all categories on or near the Via Veneto or at the top of the Spanish

Ancient Roman statues stand now on the Campidoglio

Steps. But if being in a fashionable neighborhood is less important to you than the comforts of a brand-new hotel in a convenient location, the hotels near the central railroad station are likely to please you more. The neighborhood hasn't the charm of other areas, but some of Rome's best buys in the way of up-to-date, air-conditioned hotels are there.

If you would like to put up in the midst of old Rome, surrounded by narrow cobblestoned streets, old palaces, and open-air markets, choose the Pantheon-Piazza Montecitorio section. The atmosphere of Rome is at its most typical there, the hotels are comfortable, and you are within walking distance of many of the city's most famous landmarks.

If you plan to do a lot of shopping and want to be within walking distance of many of Rome's justly celebrated shops, the Piazza di Spagna-Corso section is the most central in Rome. The neighborhood near Piazza del Popolo is several blocks away from the shopping section but somewhat quieter.

If your chief interest is St. Peter's and the Vatican, the hotels in the St. Peter's-Prati area are for you. Last of all, if you have a car, a good solution may be the Parioli or Nomentana or Salaria sections. These are all pleasant residential neighborhoods and, being away from the center of town, are considerably quieter and more restful. It is, of course, much easier to park in these sections than in the middle of town, and the hotels represent extremely good value since most of them are new, attractive, and not too expensive.

HOTEL OR PENSION?

Most of the places listed as "inexpensive" in the following directory are pensions rather than hotels. Americans are not as familiar with this type of accommodation as they should be. The chief difference between a pension and a hotel is that the pension is usually smaller and the price of your meals is included in the price of the room. Almost without exception the food is excellent and abundant.

A building in the new University City

Street scene, Via Margutta

If you prefer, it is often possible to arrange to have *mezza pensione* (half-pension) which means you take only one meal there in addition to breakfast. Ordinarily you need not specify which meal you will take at the pension, which makes it easier to plan your day's activities. Pensions are particularly recommended for a longer stay, since they are smaller and less formal than hotels and since weekly rates can be arranged. You will appreciate the informal atmosphere, particularly if you are traveling with children.

You should remember, too, that many hotels, particularly at the height of the tourist season, insist that guests take their meals there. Not all visitors take happily to this arrangement. Eating at a hotel, in contrast to having your meals at a pension, is no economy. And hotel food, all too often, is the uninspired kind of "international cuisine" that seems to have been designed primarily to avoid offending any palate. Since one of the highlights for most visitors to Rome is the discovery of the excellent food and the delightful atmosphere of the Roman restaurants, many tourists are understandably reluctant to be limited to a single eating place.

PRICES AND SERVICE CHARGES

The hotels listed in the following pages have been divided into four categories: *De Luxe, First Class, Moderate Priced,* and *Inexpensive.* Within the limitations of their classes, all of them have a considerable range of prices. In actual practice, however, during the busy tourist season you are very likely to be asked the maximum rate or something near it. The rates shown below for each category are based on the official government listing at the time this guide went to press. The first figure is an average of the maximum permissible *base rate* for a single room with and without bath, and for a double room with and without bath. The figures below are the approximate rates, in lire and dollars, *including service charge (18%) and the various taxes.* Obviously there will be some individual variations from this average, but you will find that in general prices run about as follows:

	Single with bath	Double with bath	Single without bath	Double without bath
De Luxe	*13,000 l.* *50,000 l.—$50*	*22,000 l.* *45,500 l.—$70*	None	None
First Class	*10,000 l.* *21,500 l.—$33*	*16,000 l.* *24,000 l.—$37*	None	None
Moderate	*5,800 l.* *10,500 l.—$16*	*9,000 l.* *16,200 l.—$25*	*4,000 l.* *7,800 l.—$12*	*7,500 l.* *10,000 l.—$17*
Inexpensive	*4500 l.* *7,800 l.—$12*	*6,500 l.* *10,500 l.—$16*	*3,200 l.* *4,500 l.—$7*	*5,200 l.* *7,800 l.—$12*

For De Luxe and First Class hotels, the prices quoted above generally include everything, including the tax (which for reasons perhaps not even known to the Italians can sometimes be slightly higher than the usual 18%), service, and breakfast. In Moderate Priced and Inexpensive hotels, the price quoted here (and by the hotels themselves) is more likely to represent a base rate, with tax, service, etc., added on separately. In some hotels there is an additional charge for air-conditioning or heating, varying from 2000–3000 lire ($1.50–$3.00) per night.

When you register at a hotel, you will do well to ask the price of your room *tutto compreso* (all-inclusive). By doing that you will eliminate a good deal of involved (and perhaps inaccurate) mental arithmetic and avoid unpleasant surprises. If you have any question about what your room should cost, remember that by law the price must be posted in each room. You will usually find it on the back of the door. If in doubt, ask.

Special Note. The prices quoted here are the official prices at the time this book went to press. They may have been increased by the time you read this. It is more than likely, for example, that during the time of an international conference in Rome they will be much higher. If you plan to visit Rome at such a time, be sure to check the prices beforehand with your travel agent.

TIPPING

For an overnight stay in a hotel you need not worry about tipping, except for the bellboy who carries your bags. He should be tipped at least 200 lire in an inexpensive hotel and at least 500 lire in an expensive hotel. If you stay longer, you will want to tip the *portiere* (the French call him *concierge*), who takes care of your messages, gets you theater and train tickets, sends telegrams for you, supplies you with a variety of useful information, and generally smooths your path. Since he bills you separately for tickets, telegrams, or whatever he has arranged for you, you can figure his tip at 10% or 15% of his bill. The chambermaid should also be given a small tip, varying, in a luxury hotel, from 500 to 1,000 lire, depending upon the length of your stay.

One of the formal gardens in Vatican City

VIA VENETO, PIAZZA BARBERINI, AND VICINITY

DE LUXE

Ambasciatori, Via Vittorio Veneto 70. Quietly elegant hotel just across from the American Embassy. Outdoor dining terrace in summer. Air conditioning. 152 rooms.

Bernini-Bristol, Piazza Barberini 23. Faces the Triton Fountain in one of the city's busiest squares. Luxurious, but commercial atmosphere. Air conditioning. 133 rooms.

Eden, Via Ludovisi 49. Overlooking the Borghese Gardens a short walk from Via Veneto. Its roof garden at cocktail time has a magnificent view of Rome. 117 rooms.

Excelsior, Via Vittorio Veneto 125. An old standby and favorite of American film stars, buyers, and convention-goers. Air conditioning. 395 rooms.

Flora, Via Vittorio Veneto 191. At the Porta Pinciana gate, close to the entrance to the Borghese Gardens. Air conditioning. 177 rooms.

Hassler, Piazza Trintà dei Monti 6. At the top of the Spanish Steps and close to the Borghese Gardens. Its roof top restaurant is famous for the view. Air conditioning. 98 rooms.

FIRST CLASS

Anglo-Americano, Via Quattro Fontane 12. Near the Barberini Palace and just off Piazza Barberini. 115 rooms.

Boston, Via Lombardia 47. On a quiet street a short walk from Via Veneto. Slightly old-fashioned but pleasant. 121 rooms.

De la Ville. Via Sistina 69. Near the top of the Spanish Steps and close to the Borghese Gardens. 183 rooms.

Eliseo, Via di Porta Pinciana 30. Just off Via Veneto, near the Pinciana gate. Roof-top restaurant. 60 rooms.

Jolly, Corso d'Italia 1. Rome's newest centrally located hotel. Ultra-modern. Garage. Air conditioning. 169 rooms.

Majestic, Via Vittorio Veneto 50. On the tree-shaded lower part of Via Veneto, close to Piazza Barberini. 100 rooms.

Regina Carlton, Via Vittorio Veneto 72. Slightly old-fashioned, quiet hotel just across from the American Embassy. 134 rooms.

Imperiale, Via Vittorio Veneto 24. Slightly old-fashioned hotel not far from Piazza Barberini. 84 rooms.

Savoia, Via Ludovisi 15. Just off Via Veneto, near the American Consulate. 110 rooms.

Victoria, Via Campania 41. Newly modernized hotel near the Pinciana gate. 110 rooms.

MODERATE PRICED

Caprice, Via Liguria 38. Small hotel just off Via Veneto. 25 rooms, all with bath.

Residenza, La, Via Emilia 22. Small quiet pension, one block from Via Veneto. 28 rooms.

Inghilterra, Via Bocca di Leone 14. Old-fashioned hotel near the Piazza di Spagna much favored by experienced travelers. 94 rooms.

Internazionale, Via Sistina 79. Small hotel near the top of the Spanish Steps. 35 rooms.

Alexandra, Via Veneto 18. Friendly, well run hotel near Piazza Barberini. 44 rooms.

INEXPENSIVE

Bellavista Milton (pension), Via di Porta Pinciana 16-a. Near Via Veneto, overlooking the Borghese Gardens. 52 rooms.

Dinesen, Via di Porta Pinciana 18. Family-style hotel in what used to be an old monastery. Excellent food. 32 rooms.

Santa Elisabetta (pension), Via Vittorio Veneto 146. Small and quiet, yet close to the action. 10 rooms.

Tea (pension), Via Sardegna 149. Modern pension a few blocks from Via Veneto. 32 rooms.

Villa Borghese (pension), Via Giovanni Sgambati 4. Charming pension across from the Borghese Gardens. Outdoor dining in summer. 15 rooms.

PIAZZA DI SPAGNA, VIA DEL CORSO, PIAZZA DEL POPOLO

FIRST CLASS

Marini Strand, Via del Tritone 17. Near the busy crossroads of Largo Chigi. 114 rooms.

Plaza, Via del Corso 126. At the heart of the main shopping center. 207 rooms.

MODERATE PRICED

King Hotel, Via Sistina 131. Well located between Via Veneto and Piazza di Spagna, 61 rooms.

Lugano, Via del Tritone 132. On one of Rome's busiest streets, in the center of town. 34 rooms.

Regno, Via del Corso 330. Near Piazza Colonna, in the heart of the business section. 26 rooms.

INEXPENSIVE

Croce di Malta, Via Borgognona 28. On a side street parallel to fashionable Via Condotti. 26 rooms.

Cecil, Via Francesco Crispi 55-c. On busy street, near everything. Ibsen once lived here. 28 rooms.

Madrid, Via Mario dei Fiori 93. Centrally located, four blocks from Piazza di Spagna. 36 rooms.

City, (pension), Via Due Macelli 97. A few steps from the Piazza di Spagna and American Express. 28 rooms.

RAILROAD TERMINAL VIA NÁZIONALE, AND VICINITY

DE LUXE

Grand, Via Vittorio Emanuele Orlando 3. Spacious, dignified hotel with old-world atmosphere. Air conditioning. 177 rooms.

Mediterraneo, Via Cavour 15. Large modern hotel near the railroad station. All double rooms are with bath. Air conditioning. 272 rooms.

FIRST CLASS

Atlantico, Via Cavour 23. Modern, comfortable hotel near the railroad station. All double rooms are with bath. Air conditioning. 83 rooms.

Continentale, Via Cavour 5. Slightly old-fashioned but comfortable hotel near the railroad station. 270 rooms.

Commodore, Via Torino 1. Modern, well run. Garage. Air conditioning. 65 rooms.

Forum, Via Tor de'Conti 25–30. Charming, small. Overlooks the Forum of Augustus. Roof garden. Air conditioning. 76 rooms.

Royal Santina, Via Marsala 22. New, all conveniences. Garage. Air conditioning. 121 rooms.

Universo, Via Principe Amedeo 5. Comfortable and new. Garage. Air conditioning. 206 rooms.

Massimo d'Azeglio, Via Cavour 18. Modern, comfortable hotel near the railroad station. Air conditioning. 209 rooms.

Metropole, Via Principe Amedeo 5. Modern, comfortable hotel near the railroad station. Air conditioning. 285 rooms, all with bath.

Quirinale, Via Nazionale 7. Pleasant, slightly old-fashioned hotel on one of Rome's main shopping streets. 189 rooms.

Reale, Via Venti Settembre 30. Quiet, slightly old-fashioned hotel near Piazza San Bernardo. 82 rooms.

San Giorgio, Via Giovanni Amendola 61. Comfortable hotel near the railroad station. Air conditioning. 186 rooms.

MODERATE PRICED

Alpi, Via Castelfidardo 84-A. Small and quiet, yet near everything. 34 rooms.

Rex, Via Torino 149. Comfortable and well located. All rooms with bath or shower and breakfast included. 54 rooms.

Siviglia, Via Gaeta 12. Intimate and tranquil. Garage. 31 rooms.

Sorrento-Patrizia, Via Nazionale 251. On one of the city's main thoroughfares, within walking distance of practically everywhere. 85 rooms.

Esperia, Via Nazionale 22. On one of Rome's main shopping streets. 94 rooms.

Lux, Via Volturno 36. Not far from the railroad station. 103 rooms.

Nizza, Via Massimo d'Azeglio 16. Near the railroad station. 63 rooms.

Nord-Nuova Roma, Via Giovanni Amendola 3. Near the railroad station. 164 rooms.

Pace Elvezia, Via Quattro Novembre 104. Near Piazza Venezia. 64 rooms.

San Remo, Via Massimo d'Azeglio 36. Near the railroad station. 72 rooms.

Sitea (pension), Via Vittorio Emanuele Orlando 90. Near Piazza Esedra. 26 rooms.

INEXPENSIVE

Adria, (pension), Via XX Settembre 58. 18 rooms.

Dell'Opera, Via Principe Amedeo 14. All but a few rooms with bath. Near the opera. 24 rooms.

Dorica (pension), Piazza Viminale 14. Near the Teatro dell'Opera. All double rooms are with bath. 13 rooms.

Igea, Via Principe Amedeo 97. Near the railroad station. 42 rooms.

Medici, Via Flavia 96. Not far from the Piazza San Bernardo. 59 rooms.

PANTHEON, PIAZZA MONTECITORIO, AND VICINITY

DE LUXE

Parco dei Principi, Via Frescobaldi. Very Hollywood. Palms, outdoor grill, pool. Overlooks the Borghese Park. 203 rooms.

FIRST CLASS

Residence Palace, Via Archimede 69. Rooms and housekeeping suites in the fashionable Parioli residential section. 191 rooms, all with bath.

Beverly Hills, Largo Benedetto Marcello 220. Near the beginning of Via Salaria. All rooms with baths. New and well equipped. 172 rooms.

Milano, Piazza Montecitorio 12. Just behind Piazza Colonna, in the heart of the city. 90 rooms.

Minerva, Piazza della Minerva 69. Near the Pantheon. 180 rooms.

Nazionale, 131 Piazza Montecitorio. Excellent service. In the heart of Rome and a favorite of government officials. 100 rooms.

Raphael, Largo Febo 2. Intimate and elegant and off the beaten path, yet in the very heart of Old Rome. Air conditioning. 85 rooms.

Hermitage, Via Eugenio Vajna 12. On a tree-lined residential street. Well run, all conveniences. Air conditioning. 100 rooms.

Claridge, Viale Liegi 62. Just far enough from the center to be a restful retreat. Garages. Air conditioning. 89 rooms.

Ritz Presidential, Piazza Euclide 43. Pleasant, peaceful and modern. Out of the city's center. 116 rooms.

MODERATE PRICED

Bologna, Via Santa Chiara 4/A. Near the Pantheon. 122 rooms.

Cesari, Via di Pietra 89/A. In the midst of old Rome, near the heart of the city. 51 rooms.

Genio, Via Giuseppe Zanardelli 28. Near Piazza Navona. 65 rooms.

Senato, Piazza della Rotonda 73. Near the Pantheon. 54 rooms.

Sole al Pantheon, Piazza del Pantheon 63. Situated in a 14th c. palazzo in one of the most beautiful squares in Rome. 33 rooms.

PARIOLI, NOMENTANA, SALARIA, AND VICINITY

Garden Roxy, Piazza B. Gastaldi 4. New hotel in the fashionable Parioli residential section. 55 rooms.

Fleming, Piazza Monteleone di Spoleto. In the fashionable Fleming residential area. Good service and good food at a good price. Parking. Air conditioning. 282 rooms.

Parioli, Viale Bruno Buozzi 54. Modern, attractive hotel in the Parioli residential section. 89 rooms.

Rivoli, Via Taramelli 7. Modern. unpretentious; off Viale Bruno Buozzi, in the Parioli section. 47 rooms.

Villa degli Aranci, Via Barnaba Oriani 11. Hotel with garden in a quiet residential neighborhood. 46 rooms.

INEXPENSIVE

Delle Muse (pension), Via Tommaso Salvini 18. On a quiet residential street near the edge of the city. 42 rooms.

Paisiello Parioli (pension), Via Paisiello 47. Attractive pension a short bus ride from the center of town. 35 rooms.

Villa del Parco (pension), Via Nomentana 110. In the tree-shaded Nomentana section. 23 rooms.

ST. PETER'S, PRATI, AND VICINITY

FIRST CLASS

Michelangelo, Via Stazione di San Pietro 14. New, modern hotel. All rooms are with bath. Air conditioning. 150 rooms.

Giulio Cesare, Via degli Scipioni 287. Excellent small hotel on a quiet street near the Tiber and St. Peter's. 65 rooms.

Leonardo da Vinci, 324 Via dei Gracchi. Modern, quiet, well run. Two restaurants, American bar, famous barbershop, garage. 264 rooms.

MODERATE PRICED

Alicorni, Via Scossacavalli 11. Close to St. Peter's. 45 rooms.

Columbus, Via della Conciliazione 33. Near St. Peter's. Unusual decoration. 104 rooms.

Olimpic, Via Properzio 2/A. In the Prati section, not far from Castel Sant'Angelo. 77 rooms.

INEXPENSIVE

Casa di Provvidenza, Via Giovanni Prati 1. Modest but nice. Friendly owners. 34 rooms.

OUTSKIRTS OF ROME

DE LUXE

Cavalieri Hilton, Via Cadlolo, Monte Mario. Spectacular view of the city. 400 rooms.

Helio Cabala, Via Spinabella, Marino. Fifteen miles from Rome. Two pools, terrace restaurants, good decor. Rooms, suites, and villas. 40 rooms.

FIRST CLASS

Americana di Roma, Via Aurelia (at 16 km. mark from Rome). On a quiet hill off the highway. Pool. Air conditioning. 89 rooms.

Caesar Augustus, Corso Francia 200. Modern. Open-air pool, roof restaurant. Air conditioning. 105 rooms.

Eurogarden, Via Salaria (12 km.). Near Autostrada del Sole. Quiet. 40 Rooms.

La Villa (pension), Via del Pescaccio 101 (10.5 km. near the Raccordo Anulare). Quiet, isolated. Tennis and swimming. 34 rooms.

Holiday Inn, Via Aurelia Antica 415. Just inside city limits. Restaurant, snack bar, hairdresser, pool. Air conditioning. 335 rooms.

MODERATE

Autostello A.C.I., Via C. Columbo (13 km. from Rome). Excellent motel. Midway between Rome and airport. Pool, garages. 72 rooms.

Bela, Via Cassia (18 km.). Motel, tranquil setting. 40 rooms.

EUR, Via Pontina (5 km.). Small, quiet motel. 22 rooms.

INEXPENSIVE

AGIP, Via Aurelia (8.4 km.). Motel on a hillside 15 minutes drive from St. Peter's. 132 rooms.

Boomerang, Via Aurelia (10 km. from Rome). American style motel. Gardens, pool. 40 rooms.

CHAPTER *6*

WHAT TO EAT AND WHERE

Eating is no problem in Rome, although keeping your figure may be. Food is carefully chosen, prepared with care, and served attentively in even the simplest restaurants in the city. It's not impossible to eat badly in Rome—but it's unlikely.

HOW TO EAT WELL

The first rule for eating well is to forget what you think you know about Italian food. Contrary to what many people expect, Italians use very little garlic in cooking. Most dishes have none at all, and where it is used it is added with a very light touch. Teen-agers may be surprised to learn that spaghetti and meatballs is not an Italian dish at all and they won't find it listed on the menu of any genuine Italian restaurant, although some of the American-style luncheon-ettes occasionally serve it.

The second rule is to eat at Roman meal hours, and for most Americans that's not quite so easy. Romans lunch and dine late and you may need to sustain yourself with a mid-morning or mid-after-noon snack. That, by the way, is one reason for the number of cafés you see. Don't be alarmed at the sight of so many BAR signs; many of these places sell nothing more alcoholic than a very mild *apéritif,* though they commonly do a thriving business in coffee, soft drinks, sandwiches, pastries, and ice cream, with which the Romans bridge the long gaps between meals.

If you try to keep to your regular meal hours in Rome, you'll find yourself eating in empty restaurants, which is depressing regardless of the quality of the food. Lunchtime for most Romans is at about

New apartments in a modern section of Rome

1:30, though restaurants usually serve lunch between 12:30 and 2:30. Dinner is at about 9 or 9:30; restaurants start serving at about 8, ending at about 10:30.

The third rule is to eat what the Romans eat and, if you can manage it, the way they eat it. This doesn't necessarily mean a virtuoso performance with the spaghetti fork, but it does mean that you should eat spaghetti or other *pasta* dishes as a separate course before the meat course—never as a side dish with the meat.

The fourth rule is not to be in a hurry. Food is prepared to order in Italy and it's well worth waiting a few minutes for it. Very little canned or frozen food is used; and since the whole menu has not been lurking coyly on steam tables, you may have to wait for the dishes you order. Italians look on their meal hours as leisurely, relaxing times and don't mind waiting a little while for the food to arrive. When you're through eating, don't expect to find the check on the table. The waiter will courteously allow you to sit at the table and chat as long as you like, without ostentatiously pacing back and forth or inquiring if you'd like the bill. When you're finally ready to go, ask the waiter for the check (*il conto*), or signal him by making a scribbling motion with your hand—an international sign language he'll immediately understand.

WHAT TO EAT

As befits a capital city, Rome has restaurants serving the specialties of nearly all the regions of Italy. You will find dishes *alla Bolognese, alla Fiorentina, alla Napolitana, alla Milanese,* and *alla Genovese* on menus throughout the city. But Rome also boasts its own food specialties as well. Romans claim that their cooking, striking a happy balance, is the best in Italy; it is more highly flavored than the Florentine and less heavy than the Neapolitan.

One of the best-known Roman *pasta* dishes (*pasta* includes the whole spaghetti-noodle-dumpling family) is *fettuccine all'uovo,* medium-width egg noodles, served either with only butter and cheese or with sauce and cheese. Other *pasta* favorites are spaghetti *alla carbonara* (with bacon and egg), spaghetti *alla matriciana* (with a spicy

A cafe on the elegant Via Veneto

A road near Castel Gandolfo

sauce of tomatoes, onions, and bacon), *gnocchi alla Romana* (potato dumplings with tomato sauce and cheese or with just butter and cheese), and *gnocchi di semolina* (made of farina and baked with butter and cheese). Traditionally, *gnocchi* are served on Thursdays in Roman restaurants. Many restaurants feature *cannelloni,* which are delectable stuffed tubular pancakes, covered with sauce and baked. A few restaurants serve *pizza* as one of their *pasta* dishes but only as part of a dinner and not as a meal in itself. If you want just a *pizza* and perhaps a salad, go to a *pizzeria* and not a regular restaurant. (And please don't say "pizza pie." *Pizza* means pie.)

Once you emerge from the *pasta,* it's time to consider the meat specialties. Most famous is probably *abbacchio alla Romana,* which is roast young lamb, flavored with herbs and frequently with a touch of garlic. Warning: it's a flavorful dish, but because of the small size of the lamb and the way the meat is cut, you may find yourself faced with more bones and fat than you are used to coping with. *Pollo alla diavola* is chicken, rubbed with herbs and pepper and grilled on a spit. Roman chickens are small and so an average portion is half a chicken. In addition to lamb and chicken, there are all the veal dishes that are Italian classics—*vitello arrosto* (roast veal), *cotoletta alla Milanese* (breaded veal cutlet), *lombatine di vitello* (grilled veal chop), and many others. *Saltimbocca alla Romana* is another specialty of the city and consists of thin slices of veal wrapped around a small piece of ham, flavored with sage or other herbs and sometimes with moz-zarella cheese on top. Still another favorite is *filetto di tacchino* (sliced breast of turkey), sautéed in butter and served sometimes with new peas, sometimes with mushrooms, sometimes with truffles.

If you want steak, the best idea is to go to one of the restaurants specializing in Florentine cooking which literally "import" their beef from the area around Florence. The steaks are not so thick as Ameri-can ones but the flavor is excellent.

Fish, too, is good in Rome since the city is very close to the sea. The specific varieties are different from Atlantic fish with which you are familiar but are well worth closer acquaintance. You may have them roasted, broiled, or poached and served with olive oil and lemon juice; or cold and served with homemade mayonnaise. *Zuppa di cozze,* in season, is a hearty dish of mussels cooked in broth. (You sop up the remaining liquid with bread after disposing of the mussels.) Many restaurants feature spaghetti *alle vongole* (spaghetti with clam sauce) on Fridays. For the more adventurous, *fritto di scampi e calamaretti* (fried shrimp and baby squid) is a very popular dish; and if you will forget whatever it is you think that you think about squid, you will probably enjoy it. *Calamaretti* have a delicate nut-like flavor that seems to be enhanced by deep-fat frying.

When it comes to vegetables, Roman peas (*piselli*) are well known everywhere. They are tiny, young, and tender, cooked sometimes with *prosciutto* (Italian ham) for a favorite vegetable and meat combination. But the vegetable for which Rome is famous throughout Italy is the artichoke (*carciofo*). Artichokes in Rome are like artichokes nowhere else. They have little in common with the huge, tough-leaved American variety and are barely on speaking terms with the French version. Picked when small and tender, Roman artichokes are served in a limitless variety of ways and every delectable bit is edible. You can have *carciofi alla Romana,* prepared with a little garlic, herbs, and olive oil; you can have them *alla giudea*—sliced crosswise and deep-fat fried to golden crispness; you can have them in an omelette, either hot or cold (*frittata di carciofi*). However you have them, they are always good.

In spring, asparagus is served in a number of appealing ways. You first decide whether you want *asparagi di campo* (very slender field asparagus) or *asparagi di giardino* (garden asparagus). You may have it with butter and Parmesan cheese, with a poached egg on top, or cold with olive oil and lemon juice (*all'agro*). As a matter of fact, Romans eat many cooked vegetables cold *all'agro* in salads. *Fagiolini* (string beans), *spinaci* (spinach), *cicoria* (chicory), *broccoletti* (broccoli, but much leafier than the American variety) and *zucchini* (zucchini) all lend themselves happily to this treatment.

Dessert for Romans nearly always means fruit. In season, the little wild strawberries (*fragoline*) from the Alban Hills or the big strawberries (*fragolone*) are served in all sorts of ways—except with cream. You can have strawberries with lemon juice and sugar, with orange

Via Appia Antica

Rocca Di Papa and the valley below

juice and sugar, with Marsala wine, or even with vanilla ice cream. Mixed fruit (*macedonia*) is always available and caramel custard usually is too. Some Romans like *finocchio* (a licorice-flavored, celery-like raw vegetable) for dessert. In winter some restaurants serve a *Monte Bianco* for dessert, which is a luscious, calory-jammed concoction of whipped cream and puréed chestnuts in baked meringue. An all-year-round dessert is the *delizioso,* which is a rather heavy almond cake. Sweets certainly are not lacking, but nine Romans out of ten prefer fresh fruit for dessert. And they eat it with a knife and fork.

WHAT TO DRINK

The water in Rome is good and you can drink it freely; but many Italians, who consider themselves connoisseurs of water, prefer mineral water for its flavor. There are many types, both naturally carbonated and still, and some travelers recommend sticking to one or two brands of mineral water while traveling to avoid those unfortunate difficulties often blamed on "change of water."

While we're on the subject of water, you'd better be warned that what is called soda water in the United States is called *"seltz"* in Italy. If you want scotch and soda, ask for scotch *"con seltz."* If you ask for it with soda, you have a fifty-fifty chance of being given something that tastes like bicarbonate of soda. (Won't do you any harm, but your drink will taste pretty odd.) Most hotel barmen know that Americans mean *"seltz"* when they say "soda," but at a smaller bar you may get the wrong thing.

Water is all very well, but wine with your meal costs little in Rome and complements Italian cooking even better. The more expensive

Dining at the Villa dei Pini amid the famous pines

restaurants have a wine list to choose from, but even the less expensive ones will have some of the well-known bottled wines such as Soave and Orvieto (light, dry, white wines), Verdicchio (slightly more astringent), and various kinds of red wine. In medium- and lower-priced restaurants, however, it's more economical and frequently more convenient to order *vino sciolto* (unbottled wine), which is served in a flask. The smallest-size flask is a *quartino* (about 1/2 pint), an adequate amount for a person who is not extremely thirsty. A *mezzo litro* holds a pint; and a *litro* holds a full liter, which is slightly more than a quart. Some restaurants, instead of using small flasks, will put a large bottle on the table and charge for as much as is consumed. *Vino sciolto* is Rome—whether it is Frascati from the Alban Hills, Nettuno from the area near Anzio, or Maccarese from the vineyards north of Rome—is usually good and is very inexpensive. A *quartino* generally costs about 150 lire—about 25 cents.

In the interest of amity between nations, try to stick to wine, beer, or water with your meals. Italians are puzzled and almost offended at the sight of tourists having soft drinks with their meals. They feel that somehow it is an affront to their cooking.

RISTORANTE VS. TRATTORIA

A *ristorante* is generally more elaborate and more expensive than a *trattoria,* although some of the most famous eating places in Rome pride themselves on being called *trattoria.* A *trattoria* is usually less pretentious than a *ristorante* and frequently less formal, but it is clean, the food is good, and the atmosphere is friendly. In the listing which follows there are representatives of both types.

A *tavola calda* is the Italian version of a quick-lunch counter, where you can eat a variety of cold or hot dishes quickly and economically.

WHAT IT COSTS

Although food, particularly meat, is relatively expensive in Rome, other costs are low and so a good restaurant meal will cost a great deal less than a comparable one in a city such as New York. If you like luxurious surroundings and elaborate food, you can pay as much as 13,000 lire ($20.00) or more per person in Rome—but you can also eat extremely well for a fraction of that. The average price for a good meal in a very expensive restaurant is about 10,000 lire ($15.00) per person, but you can have an excellent dinner for 4,000 lire ($6.25) and a very good one for even less.

Restaurant prices include more than the food. All restaurants have a small cover charge, which may be as low as 50 lire in a small *trattoria* but is likely to be about 100 lire in an average restaurant. There is also a service charge, which is a percentage added on to the total, and a tax. The service charge varies between 10% and 17% of the bill, depending on the classification of the restaurant.

In the following list, restaurants are classified as de luxe, moderately priced, and inexpensive. Although, of course, the cost of the meal will vary with what you order, in general you can figure that a meal for one at a de luxe restaurant will cost between 8,000 and 11,000 lire ($12.50 to $17.00). A dinner at a moderate-priced restaurant will cost between 3,500 and 4,500 lire ($5.50 to $7.00), and a meal at an inexpensive restaurant will come to between 2,000 and 2,500 lire ($3.00 to $4.00).

Many of the moderate-priced and inexpensive restaurants have a fixed-price dinner, for approximately 2,000 lire, not including beverage. Usually you must ask for this special menu, however, since most restaurants would prefer to have you order a la carte.

The National Gallery of Modern Art

VIA VENETO, PIAZZA BARBERINI, VILLA BORGHESE, AND VICINITY

DE LUXE

Capriccio, Via Liguria 38. Pleasant intimate dining. Bar and terrace in summer.

Casina Valadier, Villa Borghese. A quietly old-fashioned restaurant whose terrace, overlooking the Pincio, has a magnificent view of the city, best seen at lunchtime. There is also an outdoor cafe, popular both in the morning and at teatime.

George's, Via Marche 7. (Closed in August.) International cuisine in an elegant, intimate restaurant with a small garden. Good bar, unusual food.

Sans Souci, Via Sicilia 20. Elegant and intimate. First rate menu, international specialties.

Taverna Flavia, Via Flavia 9. Excellent, varied menu. A favorite of the Roman aristocracy and visiting celebrities.

MEDIUM-PRICED

Al Chianti, Via Ancona 17–19. Specializing in superbly prepared game (wild boar, pheasant, quail), this restaurant is always good but is particularly inviting during the fall hunting season.

Giggi Fazi "Giardino d'Inverno," Via Lucullo 22. Hearty Roman specialties such as *rigatoni*, as well as meat broiled on a revolving spit. Pleasant garden for summer dining.

Gino, Via Rasella 52. Florentine steaks and a garlic-flavored bean soup are featured in an unpretentious setting. Roman theater and movie personalities dine here frequently.

Sergio e Ada, Via del Boccaccio 1 (corner of Via Rasella). A husband and wife team that has been going strong for years turn out food typical of the Roman kitchen at its best.

Piccolo Mondo, Via Aurora 39/d. This pleasant, always crowded trattoria has quadrupled in size over the last ten years because the food is good and the owner very *simpatico*.

PIAZZA VENEZIA, LARGO ARGENTINA, AND VICINITY

MEDIUM-PRICED

La Carbonara, 23 Piazza Campo de' Fiori. Famous for spaghetti alla carbonara.

Angelino, Piazza Margana. Outdoor dining in summer in a tiny Roman square that looks like an opera setting.

Taverna Giulia, Vicolo dell'Oro 23. An attractive, restful retreat at the beginning of the historic Via Giulia. Warmly inviting in winter; outdoor dining in summer. French-Italian cooking.

Piperno, Via Monte Cenci 9. Another *trattoria* in the old ghetto section, famous for its *carciofi alla giudia* (crisp fried artichokes) and *filetto di baccala* (deep-fried puffy codfish filets).

Ulpia, Piazza Foro Traiano 2. Night club-restaurant in history-packed location, overlooking Trajan's Market.

INEXPENSIVE

Giggetto, Via del Portico di Ottavia 21/A. Unpretentious *trattoria* with good food, in the heart of the old Roman ghetto, within sight of the Theater of Marcellus.

An unusual view of the Colosseum

PIAZZA DI SPAGNA, CORSO, PIAZZA DEL POPOLO, AND VICINITY

DE LUXE

Alfredo all'Augusteo, Piazza Augusto Imperatore 30. Famous among tourists for its *fettuccine* (egg noodles), served with a gold fork and spoon, and for flaming omelets served with a flourish.

Ranieri, Via Mario dei Fiori 26. Elegantly Victorian restaurant proud of its tradition of fine French-Italian cooking.

Toula' Di Roma, Via della Lupa 29b. Sophisticated, luxurious. Unusual food beautifully served.

MEDIUM PRICED

da Mario, Via della Vite 55. Probably the very best trattoria in Rome. Every dish on the menu is superb, but the *stracotto* (pot roast, Florentine style), the *paté di fagiano* (pheasant paté) and the wine produced on Mario's own Tuscan land are all incomparable.

Dal Bolognese, Piazza del Popolo 1. Fine, moderately priced restaurant with outdoor terrace on one of Rome's most imposing piazzas. Cold chicken in gelatine is a summer specialty; baked green noodles and other Bolognese dishes are served all year round.

La Fontanella, Largo Fontanella di Borghese 86. Famous among Roman socialites for steak and other Florentine specialties.

Otello, Via della Croce 81. A stone's throw from the Spanish steps, this restaurant is especially charming in summer, when you can dine on the well-cooked Roman dishes in a cool vine-covered courtyard.

La Lampara, Via della Penna 23. Pretty and relaxing. Between the Piazza del Popolo and the Tiber. Streetside dining in summer.

Nino, 11 Via Borgognona. Good steaks—a rarity in Rome.

Le Cave di S. Ignazio, Piazza S. Ignazio 169. A bit cramped, but memorable pasta, chocolate soufflé, and piazza setting.

PIAZZA COLONNA, TREVI FOUNTAIN, AND VICINITY

MEDIUM-PRICED

Al Moro, Vicolo delle Bollette 13. In a tiny passageway just off the Trevi Fountain. Many Romans swear that spaghetti *alla Moro* (with egg and bacon) is the best in town, and Moro himself agrees. *Scampi alla Moro* (broiled shrimp) are also a specialty.

Hostaria SS. Apostoli, Piazza SS. Apostoli. Specialties of the Abruzzi region served in a quiet, gracious atmosphere.

INEXPENSIVE

La Capricciosa, Largo Lombardi 8. Cheerful, comfortable. Outside dining in summer. Anything from pizza to full-course meal.

PANTHEON, PIAZZA NAVONA, AND VICINITY

DE LUXE

Alfredo alla Scrofa, Via della Scrofa 104. The "other" Alfredo and equally famous for *fettuccine* and other dishes. Somewhat more intimate atmosphere. (*Fettuccine* fanciers try them both.)

Hostaria dell'Orso, Via Monte Brianzo 93. Handsome upstairs night club-restaurant in a beautiful old Renaissance palace. The setting is at least as impressive as the food, but it is one of Rome's most elegant night spots.

Passetto, Via Giuseppe Zanardelli 12. Chic modern restaurant with a large summer terrace, just off Piazza Navona. Specialties include *cannelloni, pizza* (but not as a main dish), and a wide variety of both Italian and international dishes.

MEDIUM-PRICED

Angoletto "da Alfredo," Piazza Rondanini 51. Very good pasta and a wide choice of roasted meats. The country-fresh vegetables are unusually good. Patio-dining in summer.

TRASTEVERE

pizzeria on the other side of the stairs). *Cannelloni,* chicken *alla diavola,* and other specialties.

Il Buco, Via Sant'Ignazio 8. Small restaurant specializing in Florentine steaks and *pappardelle al sugo di lepre* (noodles with wild rabbit).

Tre Scalini, Piazza Navona 30. Restaurant with raised terrace on one of Rome's most beautiful piazzas, the long oval Piazza Navona. The restaurant's own bar and ice-cream parlor also has tables on the *piazza.* Famous for its ice cream, particularly the *tartufo* (chocolate ice cream covered with bittersweet chocolate pieces). The bar is better than the restaurant.

INEXPENSIVE

Grappolo D'Oro, Piazza della Cancelleria 80. A great table laden with huge pans of freshly prepared specialties daily, served buffet style.

Papá Giovanni, Via dei Sediari 4 (just off the Piazza Navona). Warm, intimate, small, specializing in dishes garnished with truffles.

DE LUXE

Sabatini, Vicolo Santa Maria Trastevere 18. Facing the lovely church of Santa Maria in Trastevere whose 12th Century mosaics are illuminated at night. Superb seafood as well as Roman specialties. Go early or expect a long wait for a table.

MEDIUM-PRICED

La Cisterna, Via della Cisterna 13. Costumed waiters, songs, and "atmosphere" in a place that's "different."

Antica Pesa, Via Garibaldi 18. Roman specialties in an off-the-beaten-track restaurant with a good-sized garden in back.

Checco er Carrettiere, Via Benedetta 10. Popular spot crowded with good-humored, noisy Romans eating *dischi volanti* (flying saucers—a kind of *pasta*), spaghetti *alla carrettiera,* and other hearty specialties.

Da Meo Patacca, Piazza dei Mercanti 30. Old Roman atmosphere by the carload, although perhaps "authentic" is not quite the proper word. Amusing outdoor dining among decorated carts, wine barrels, and various other trappings.

Galeassi, Piazza Santa Maria in Trastevere 3. Large terrace on the handsome square facing the fountain. The situation is superior to the food, which is good enough but overpriced for its quality.

Corsetti, Piazza San Cosimato 27. An old Roman standby, famous for its fish, but serving meat dishes and pizza, too.

Romolo, Via Porta Settimiana 8. Pleasant small restaurant, noted particularly for its attractive garden in summer and its display of modern paintings indoors in winter.

INEXPENSIVE

Carlo in Trastevere, Via Cardinale Merry del Val 16B. Lots of room and a varied menu.

Vincenzo, Via della Lungaretta 173. Extremely simple, crowded *trattoria* specializing in excellent fish and seafood.

CARACALLA, APPIA ANTICA, AND VICINITY

DE LUXE

Cecilia Metella, Via Appia Antica 125. Garden restaurant on the old Appian Way. Specialty: *pollo alla Nerone* (chicken grilled with laurel leaves).

Escargot, Via Appia Antica 46. Rustic decor, sophisticated food and wine list.

MEDIUM-PRICED

Apuleius, Piazza del Tempio di Diana 15. Quiet, elegant restaurant in the Aventine section, decorated in old Roman style.

Horti Galateae, Via Porta San Sebastiano 5. Private, garden setting, quiet. The feeling of ancient Rome. Good food.

OUTSKIRTS OF ROME

MEDIUM-PRICED

Cucurucú, Via Capoprati 10 (near the Olympic Stadium). In summer the grilled and roasted meat specialties can be consumed in a lovely garden on the banks of the Tiber.

Ernesto alla Cassia, Via Oriolo Romano 59 (8 kilometers from Rome.) Open-air dining on an extensive terrace in open country. A large rolling table of unusual antipasto dishes is a specialty.

Il Casale, Via Flaminia (10 km. from Rome). Restored farmhouse. Huge fires in winter, dining on hillside terraces in summer. Buffet includes fine antipasto, chicken, steaks.

Tor Carbone, Via Appia Antica (6 km.). Country villa with serene, shady garden. Ask for any of Sora Rosa's specialties. You'll find them all delicious.

AMERICAN FOOD

California, Via Bissolati 56. Hamburgers, doughnuts, waffles, and other luncheonette specialties for homesick Americans.

Colony, Via Aurora 27. Hot and cold sandwiches, pancakes, pie a la mode, plus a few Americanized versions of Italian dishes.

Piccadilly, Via Barberini 2–16. Sit, stand, serve yourself, or be served. Hamburgers, hot dogs, rootbeer.

ICE CREAM

Giolitti, Via Uffici del Vicario 40 (In EUR: Viale Oceania 90). All Rome goes to Giolitti all summer long. The ice cream may be the best in the world. Incredible flavors.

CHAPTER 7

SHOPPING IN ROME

Listing the shops in Rome is like counting the flowers in the park. New ones spring up, old ones wither away, and meantime all too many are overlooked. The list that follows obviously cannot pretend to include all of the reputable, attractive, and interesting stores, or even all of the best of them. Fortunately there are many, many more, for, as all women and some men know, part of the fun of shopping is discovering new places for yourself. You can begin with this list and then set off on your own down almost any of the streets in the center of town. And, Rome being Rome, you won't be disappointed.

The most fashionable shopping streets in the city are in the area around Piazza di Spagna. Rome's most famous street of shops, Via Condotti, starts just across from the base of the Spanish Steps and ends at the busy intersection with the Via del Corso. Via Sistina and Via Gregoriana also abound with fashionable stores, and Via Frattina, Via del Corso, Via del Tritone, Via Francesco Crispi, and Via Due Macelli are all crowded with dozens of moderate-priced and expensive shops of all kinds. Via Nazionale, which runs from the Esedra Fountain near the railroad station to a few blocks from Piazza Venezia, is yet another popular shopping street. And if, after all of this, you are still interested in the chase, there are innumerable neighborhood shopping areas, many of them well worth a visit.

As in other cities, there are streets and areas where certain types of shops seem to congregate. You will notice that no antique stores have been listed here. Buying antiques is an expensive business, and it can be a very risky one unless you know the field extremely well. Nevertheless, if you are interested in browsing in antique shops, you will find that there are two localities where they vie for your attention.

View of the city with Temple of the Vestals in foreground

Along Via Babuino, from Piazza di Spagna to Piazza del Popolo, there are a number of fine antique shops; and along Via dei Coronari, a narrow old street north of Piazza Navona, are a great many more. Most of the best antique dealers in Rome are to be found on one of these two streets.

You may want to see the "flea market" at least once. It holds forth every Sunday morning, and diligent shoppers have often been known to emerge with treasures ranging all the way from a medieval altar piece to an early Louis Armstrong recording. There is junk—mounds of it—and it takes both immense patience and a knowing eye to sift one worth-while purchase out of the heaps of appalling castoffs. Bargaining is an essential part of the game here, and the seller will be alarmed and upset if you accept the first price he asks. The market occupies the Via Portuense, from the Porta Portese almost to the Trastevere railroad station, and the best way to approach it seems to be to plunge into the melee from about halfway down Viale Trastevere, which runs parallel to it. The part of the market near the Porta Portese is the least interesting since it consists mostly of new and used clothing, automobile accessories, and other items of minor interest to tourists. If you go—and you should—it's advisable to go early.

A small, pleasant, and far less overwhelming open market is held every day at Piazza della Fontanella Borghese, two blocks from the foot of Via Condotti. Here you will find old maps, prints and engravings, copper utensils, old books, and odd and astonishing bits of bric-a-brac spread over open stands in the midst of a busy square. Browsing and bargaining are actively encouraged by the merchants.

You should not assume, on the basis of your market experiences, that bargaining is the normal pastime of every shop owner. Most stores nowadays have *prezzi fissi* (fixed prices), which means what it says—no bargaining. It is still true, however, that if you make a number of purchases at one time, the shopkeeper may offer you a discount of his own accord. In general, it is wise to be somewhat wary of the little shop where, for no apparent reason, the price is lowered "especially for you." It usually means only that the price was too high to begin with—and after you have made your purchase, you'll have a nagging suspicion that it was still too high at the end. Professional comparison shoppers don't exist in Rome, so you will find a certain amount of variation in prices throughout the city. It's not much use, however, saying that you saw the same item for 500 lire less in another store. The clerk's reaction will be either to deny volubly that the items are identical—or else he will advise you briefly and confidentially to get it in the other place.

Best buys in Rome are men's pure silk neckties, which range in price from 1,500 to 4,000 lire, leather gloves (practically any glove store you see is good), leather bags, made-to-order clothes, silks, hand-made lingerie, and fine jewelry. Watches (imported from Switzerland) are also very good buys.

The shops in the following list have a reputation for quality and reliability. But in merchandising, as you well know, change can be rapid and unpredictable. Stores move, go out of business, change management, revise or eliminate their standards. You will do well to shop as wisely and carefully in these shops as you do in those of your own home town. As with restaurants, the shield following the listing indicates that the restaurant honors the American Express Credit Card.

Finally, here are a few do's and don'ts that may make your shopping easier and more enjoyable.

Don't try to return or exchange something once you've bought it—unless, of course, there is a real defect in the merchandise. The store owner isn't being unkind or unreasonable when he refuses. There are very real and very complicated tax reasons why he cannot refund your money. Shop carefully instead. The shopkeeper will not be surprised if you come back a couple of times before you decide to make a purchase. Romans usually do just that.

Don't insist on a sales slip as a receipt. An official receipt must have a tax stamp (for which you may have to pay) and that is why stores don't give them out freely. If you want to have a receipt for U.S. customs, the shop will give you a little note on the back of a card. That will be perfectly acceptable to the customs inspector.

Don't make unflattering remarks about the store or its merchandise in English to your companion. You'd be surprised how many Italians understand English—and Italians are very sensitive.

Do, if you have the time, have whatever article of clothing you may buy altered to fit or else made to your measure. Dressmakers and tailors are highly skilled in Rome and the fitting is superb.

Do buy silk instead of nylon in Rome. The United States is still ahead in the field of synthetics; it's foolish to buy them abroad unless you really have to. The Italians, on the other hand, do miracles with silk.
Do remember that Italian gold jewelry is 18 karat instead of the 14 karat usual in the United States; if you can afford it, it's better to buy solid-gold jewelry in Rome than gold-plated.

Tennis court in the Foro Italico

ALTA MODA (High Fashion)
You may find some models ready-made which will fit you with minor alterations. Otherwise, allow about ten days and at least three fittings for a made-to-measure suit or dress. It's expensive but worth it.
Alex, Via Sistina 42.
Capucci, Via Gregoriana 56.
Carosa, Piazza di Spagna 93.
Fabiani, Via Condotti 11.
Fontana, Via di San Sebastianello 6.
Galitzine, Via Vittorio Veneto 84.
Garnett, Via Sistina 46.
Gattinoni, Via Toscana 1.
Gregoriana, Via Gregoriana 46.
Lancetti, Via Condotti 61.
Emilio Pucci, Via Campania 59.
Valentino, Via Gregoriana 24.

BAGS, LEATHER GOODS
Antinori, Via Francesco Crispi 47.
Antinori, Via Vittorio Veneto 6.
Gucci, Via Condotti 8.
Franzi, Via del Corso, 404–405.
Fendi, Via Borgognona 56.
Funaro, Via delle Convertite 9.
Mannelli, Via Sistina 46.
Marifor, Via Frattina 86.
Romani, Via del Babuino 94.

BLOUSES
Bellini, Piazza di Spagna 77. *Also lingerie, linens.*
Cesari, Via Barberini 1. *You will find interesting blouses in a variety of styles, fabrics, and colors at most boutiques.*

BOOKS
Anglo-American Bookshop, Via della Vite 57. *Books in English.*
Lion Bookshop, Via del Babuino 181. *Books in English.*
Modernissima, Via della Mercede 43.
Rizzoli, Largo Chigi 15.

BOUTIQUES
Saint Laurent, Via Borgognona 40.
Maria Carolina, Piazza Navona.
Paoletta Blú, Via Borgognona 6.
Latte Miele, Via de'Baullari 19.
Valentino, Via Bocca Leone 15–18.

CAMERAS, FILMS
Abbondi, Piazza Navona 41.
D'Amico, Via San Claudio 87.
Kodak, Piazza Balduina 8.
Vasari, Via Sicilia 36.
Vasari, Via della Croce 74A.

CERAMICS, POTTERY
Tiburzio, Via Condotti 91.
Richard-Ginori, Via del Tritone 177.
Rosenthal, Via Condotti 15.

DEPARTMENT STORES
Cim, Via Venti Settembre 97/C.
Rinascente, Piazza Colonna, Piazza Fiume.
Standa, 379 Via del Corso, 62 Viale Trastevere, 173 Via Cola di Rienzo.

FABRICS
Burattini, Via Carrozze 3.
Galtrucco, Via del Tritone 18.
Maestosi, Via Balbo 39.
Marco, Via del Tritone 123.
Polidori, Via Borgognona 4/C.
Tomassini, Via Frattina 91.

GLASSWARE (DECORATIVE)
Fontana Arte, Via Condotti 25.
Venini, Via Condotti 59.

GLOVES
Anticoli, Via Barberini 70.
Barra, Via Sistina 14/A.
D'Auria, Via Due Macelli 55.
Manco, Piazza di Spagna 53.
Manco, Via Frattina 13.
Perrone, Piazza di Spagna 92.

GUNS, FISHING EQUIPMENT
Frinchillucci, Via Barberini 31.
Zucchi, Via Bissolati 31.

HAIRDRESSERS
Elizabeth Arden, Piazza di Spagna 19.
Castore & Polluce, Via del Babuino 99.
Filippo, Via Condotti 91.
Sergio Valente, Via Condotti 11.
Riccardo ai Mille Fiori, Via Vittorio Veneto 92.

HANDICRAFTS, GIFTS
Bella Copia, Via dei Coronari 8.
Myricae, Via Frattina 36. *Also fabrics, clothes.*

HATS, WOMEN'S
Mode Lida, Via Piave 59.
Ofelia, Via Gregoriana 25.

HATS, MEN'S
Argenti, Via del Corso 407.
Cappelleria Barbisio Co., Via del Tritone 198 a, Via Nazionale 168–169.
Lambardi, IV Novembre 157/b.

JEWELRY, REAL
Buccellati, Via Condotti 31.
Bulgari, Via Condotti 10.
Buzzetti, Via del Corso 155.
Menichini, Piazza di Spagna 1.
Ventrella, Via del Corso 168.

JEWELRY, COSTUME
Castelli, Via Frattina 54.
Burma, Via Condotti 27.

KNITWEAR
Aponte, Via Gesù e Maria 10.
Grandi Taglie. Via del Tritone 139.
Milo, Via Sistina 103.
Spagnoli, Via Vittorio Veneto 130. *Spagnoli sweaters are also available at shops throughout the city.*
Trico, Via Mancini 12.

LACES, VEILS
Rossati, Piazza di Spagna 52.
Venier Cesare, Via Frattina 79.

The Olympic Stadium

LINGERIE
Bellini, Piazza di Spagna 77. *Also blouses, linens.*
Bonelli, Piazza San Silvestro 33.
Cerri, Piazza di Spagna 89.
Cesari, Via Barberini 1.

MEN'S FURNISHINGS—Expensive
Angelo Vittucci, Via Bissolati 20.
Avenia, Via del Corso 164.
Battistoni, Via Condotti 61.
Brioni, Via Barberini 83–85.
Bertollini, Via Borgognona 4/F.
Cucci, Via Condotti 67.
Franceschini, Via del Corso 141.
Ibbas, Via Condotti 49.
Ibbas, Via Barberini 76.
Piatelli, Via Convertite 19, and Via Condotti 20.
Romagnoli, Via Crispi 52.
Valentino Umo, Via Condotti 12. *The important Valentino's.*
Serafini, Via Condotti 62.

MEN'S FURNISHINGS— Medium Priced
Cenci, Via Campo Marzio 4–7.
Medison, Via Propoganda 1A (Piazza di Spagna).
Satos, Via del Corso 403.

MODERN PAINTINGS (Galleries)
Galleria 88, Via Margutta 88.
Il Segno, Via Capo le Case 4.
La Medusa, Via Babuino 124.
La Nuova Pesa, 44–46 Via del Vantaggio.
L'Obelisco, Via Sistina 146.
La Salita, Via Garibaldi 86.
Marlborough, Via Gregoriana 5.
Schneider, Rampa Mignanelli 10.

OPTICAL GOODS
La Barbera, Via del Corso 162.
Bilgoraj, Via delle Convertite 20. *Also contact lenses.*
Vasari, Via Condotti 39.

PHARMACIES
Achille, Via Sistina 29. *Open nights.*
Carlo Erba, Via del Corso 145. *Open nights.*
Garinei, Piazza San Silvestro 31. *Open nights.*
Internazionale Apotheke, Piazza Barberini 49.
Lepetit, Via del Corso 418.

PRINTS, FLORENTINE BOXES, TRAYS
Casali, Piazza della Rotonda 81.
Panatta, Via Francesco Crispi 117.

Ponte Quattro Capi, old bridge to an island in the Tiber

Carnival at the Lido near Ostia

RELIGIOUS ARTICLES
Calabresi, Piazza della Minerva 77.
A. Casazza, Via Santa Chiara 39.
In addition to many shops on Via della Conciliazione near St. Peter's.

SHOES, WOMEN'S (High Style)
Albanese, Via Lazio 19.
Dal Co', Via di Porta Pinciana 16.
Ferragamo, Via Condotti 65.
Frattegiani, Via Sistina 50.
Raphael, Via Veneto 149.

SHOES, WOMEN'S (Medium Priced)
Bata, Via Due Macelli 45.
Magli, Via del Gambero 2.
Magli, Via Barberini 94.
Magli, Via Veneto 70.
Morosila, Via Francesco Crispi 113.
Varese, 108 Via del Tritone, 414 Via del Corso, 175 Via Nazionale.

SHOES, MEN'S
Bata, Via Due Macelli 45.
Raphael, 149 Via Veneto.
Magli, Via Barberini 94.
Magli, Via Veneto 70.
Marini, Via Francesco Crispi 97.

Samo, Via Vittorio Veneto 189.
Sanna, Via del Corso 483.

SILVER JEWELRY, GIFTS
Fornari, Via Frattina 71.
Jacolo, Piazza di Spagna 67.
Nessi, Via Sistina 133.
Saviotti, Via del Corso 133, 134, 135.
Tutunzi, Via Sistina 21.

SPORTSWEAR
Club Gamines, Via Maria Adelaide 6.
Giusti, 91–94 Piazza Trevi.
Rolands, Via Condotti 4.
Sportsman, Via Condotti 16.

STRAW BAGS, HATS, ETC.
Mazzoni, Via Francesco Crispi 88.

TOYS
De Sanctis, Via Vittorio Veneto 94.
Guffanti, Via Due Macelli 59/D.

WATCHES
Bandiera & Bedetti, Via del Teatro di Marcello 26.
Bedetti, Piazza San Silvestro 11.
Cairelli, Via del Corso 144.
Pelloni, Via del Corso 140.
Hausmann, Via del Corso 406.

CHAPTER 8

AROUND ROME

Rome is a solitary city. Surrounded by dozens of historic old towns, it still stands aloof and separate within its own confines. Near though they are, these neighboring towns have never been a part of Rome. Between them and the city lies a broad strip of pure Italian countryside, rolling and easy and dotted here and there with lonely Roman and medieval ruins. Going out of Rome in any direction, you are suddenly aware that you have left the city behind you, and while the dome of St. Peter's is still within sight, you are already in farm country, where broad, patterned fields sweep around isolated clusters of farmhouses. You share the highway with creaking high-wheeled carts, drawn by longhorned white oxen, and drive past peasant women carrying huge bundles in the immemorial way of their ancestors—balanced gracefully on their heads. The city you were in a few minutes ago is a century and a thousand miles away.

In the hills to the east and south of Rome, west along the Tyrrhenian coast, and north toward Tuscany and Umbria, are some of the most beautiful and historic towns of Italy. All of them are now within easy driving range of the city, and most of them can be reached handily by train or bus. However pressed you are for time, you should not think of leaving Rome until you have had at least one day to enjoy the country around it.

TIVOLI

Twenty miles east on the Via Valeria through the valley of the Aniene, Tivoli is one of the high lights. Near Tivoli, between Tivoli and Rome, are the stupendous ruins of **Hadrian's Villa**, one of the

Wall painting of an Etruscan tomb near Tarquinia

marvels of Imperial Rome and now acres of brick and marble and wide spaces of green. It is so quiet that the occasional muffled tinkle of a sheep's bell (for sheep graze here and there among the ruins, guarded by shepherds with crooks) sounds startlingly loud and sharp. The villa, which was in fact a marvelously contrived town devoted to pleasure and the good things of life, was built by Emperor Hadrian during the declining years of his life, to occupy himself and an army of parasitic friends and servants. There were theaters, baths, libraries, and living accommodations for hundreds of guests, servants, and guards. Hadrian had spent his life collecting things of beauty (and beautiful copies of unportable things) from the ends of the empire. All of these he gathered together at his villa, probably the largest monument to the Good Life ever constructed.

The size and scope of the villa as it was originally are almost impossible to believe, and hard even to imagine. Near the entrance to the grounds there is a scale-model reconstruction of this incredibly lavish palace, patiently restored by the archeologists from the shreds of evidence that lie scattered about. The villa, which is said to have been ten miles in circumference, sprawled in a confusion of elegant white marble over acres of countryside. Now there remain only mounds of green-covered brick and a few perfect pieces from the original, like the so-called *Maritime Theater,* a tiny circular columned island in the center of a quiet reflecting pool. There are a few larger pools and a fine little museum on the grounds, but the grandiose dream of the emperor has been lost forever. The level plateau on which it stood looking toward Rome is once again turning to grass and green vines. There are those who feel that in ruins the villa is probably much more appealing than it ever could have been in Hadrian's day. Certainly it is a marvelous change from the noise and confusion of the city, a spot where even your thoughts seem to have echoes.

Romans—and visitors too—sometimes take a picnic lunch and a bottle of *vino* to Hadrian's Villa and in the shade of the softly crumbling ruins and with a fine view of the city in the distance, enjoy a leisurely afternoon and a quiet outdoor siesta. It makes a pleasant interlude in a visit to Rome, for there is seldom a crowd and there is a lot of room.

Theater at Hadrian's Villa

The attraction of Tivoli itself, however, is the famed **Villa d'Este**, an elaborate Baroque fantasy of gardens and fountains and running water. The villa was begun as a Benedictine convent, but in 1550 it fell into the hands of Cardinal Ippolito D'Este, a dignitary not especially noted for his asceticism, who transformed the simple convent into a sumptuous villa and grounds. The villa itself, which still has a certain monastic spareness about its rooms, poises on top of a steep hill. On the elegantly terraced, tree-covered slope before it are scores, perhaps hundreds, of spouting fountains whose dazzling plumes are created by the force of gravity on water fed from the hilltop. Both the green of the garden and the beauty of the fountains become doubly impressive when you remember how parched the surrounding country is. And nothing is wasted; after its leaping hillside display, all the water eventually rejoins the Anio River in the valley below.

The modern entrance to the garden is through the villa. From the windows and balconies you look out on a mass of trees, carefully arranged to suggest a natural forest, and you *hear* the sound of a cascade. It is as if you had suddenly entered a deep woods somewhere near a waterfall. Only when you come down from the villa and enter the garden itself do you realize that you have been delightfully fooled. The sound is not that of one great waterfall (though there are several in the garden), but the orchestration of all the fountains playing at once. And the garden, which seemed so rustic, turns out to be neatly geometric, far from sylvan. This contrast between appearance and reality reflects the whole esthetic theme of the garden—an intricate arrangement of delightful surprises.

The truth is, though, that today we enter the garden at the wrong end, just at the point that was intended to be the extraordinary climax of the whole experience. You can still enjoy the effects of the garden in the sequence in which they were planned. But to do that you must walk all the way through to what is now the end and then turn down a sloping, shaded path to an iron gate that has long been closed and locked. This is the gate the Cardinal entered with his friends after the hot and dusty ride from Rome over the sandy road which still runs outside the wall. At the gate you turn, imagining that you've just entered the garden for the first time. There is nothing remarkable to see yet, but you can hear two little wall fountains trick-

A few of the fountains at Villa d' Este

Gardens of the Villa Lancellotti in Frascati

ling sluggishly near by. It is a tiny introduction, but the sound of the fountains is as sharp as a blade. "Water will be our subject matter," they seem to say. As you walk slowly up the path, past a few more wall fountains, you begin to hear the separate sounds of larger fountains ahead. Suddenly, just at the rise of the hill, you see a single huge jet in the distance, one clear fountainhead of water leaping high above you in the air. Another step or two and the whole garden is abruptly revealed. You move from one delightful surprise to another until at the door of the villa you turn for a final look at this amusing and cleverly contrived jest. And there you reach the ultimate surprise. The whole intricate maze through which you have just passed has vanished—utterly. In its place there is only a little green forest.

The Villa d' Este is also open at night, but the experience is quite different then, for all the fountains and the paths are skillfully illuminated. Though the character of the garden is changed, this modern addition to the Cardinal's design for pixyish pleasure has been so subtly arranged that the good prelate would certainly approve.

Tivoli is not all pleasure palaces. Worth seeing, too, are the *Duomo,* a 17th-century church, which retains the Romanesque bell tower from an earlier 12th-century church on the same spot; the ruins of the *Temple of Vesta* and the *Temple of the Sibyl;* and the *Villa Gregoriana,* now a fine public park.

FRASCATI

Southeast of Rome and roughly the same distance from the city as Tivoli, is another interesting and easy trip for the visitor. One route takes you out along the old Via Appia Antica with its catacombs, ruined tombs, and ancient, rutted paving stones. Like Tivoli, Frascati perches halfway up a hill. From the town you will get a splendid view of Rome and the rolling *campagna,* and on clear days you will see, far beyond Rome, the distant glitter of the sea. With its handsome hillside situation, Frascati is a good deal cooler than the city in summer, and its well-planned public flower gardens seem always to be fresh and colorful.

There are other things to see in Frascati, too, particularly the cathedral of *St. Peter's* built in 1700 and the much older *Duomo Vecchio.* Just above the town stands the handsome (and still lived in) *Villa Aldobrandini,* which has one of the most impressive views of the city of Rome in the whole area. But the one thing for which Frascati is world famous, and justly so, is the white wine that bears its name. Italian wines, among the finest in the world, always seem to lose an indefinable something by "traveling," and it is well worth going to Frascati just to drink this excellent wine at its source. Here and there are dark little wine shops with heavy wooden tables and chairs where you can sit and sip the unspoiled and inexpensive wine of Frascati as the fortunate natives have done for centuries. And in the center of the town are several modern sidewalk cafés which serve superb views with the wine. In the fall when the grapes are brought in, Frascati enjoys a wine festival that lasts several days and nights. It comes as close to being a pagan celebration as anything you're likely to see even in this country of joyous fêtes.

Near Frascati, and easily reached from there, are several small places with histories running all the way back to the days when elegant ancient Romans used to summer there. There are a number of well-preserved ruins to prove it, too, in places like Tusculum, Monte Porzio, Catone, Monte Compatri, and Rocca Priora. Frascati itself is only a small town. These ancient villages clustered around it complete the picture of Alban communal life—Rome, the *campagna,* the towns, and the villages.

In the same direction from the city as Frascati and, in fact, almost neighbors to it, are the towns of **Grottaferrata** and **Rocca di Papa.** Grottaferrata is surrounded by vineyards (which produce another excellent local wine) and is noted for its fortress-like monastery, the *Abbazia di Grottaferrata,* founded in 1004 by Saint Nilus. Within its second countyard is the church of *S. Maria* with an 11th-century wooden door, a 12th-century *campanile,* Byzantine frescoes, and rare mosaics. Often subjected to rebuilding and restoration, S. Maria is a composite unity of objects and parts from the 11th century to our own, a kind of miniature living history of the Catholic Church from the Middle Ages onward.

View from the restaurant terrace on Monte Cavo

Rocca di Papa is a real hill town, the highest in the area, with steep, medieval streets and white, stone houses that seem on the perilous verge of tumbling down the slopes on which they are built. And, fortunately, for once there isn't a mouldering ruin or a towering cathedral to lure your attention from the town itself—for that is what you should see and remember here. Rocca di Papa is certainly the most picturesque of the Alban towns, and for those who love this countryside, that is quite enough to say.

From Rocca di Papa it is a short way, but a steep and curvy one, to one of the highest inhabited spots around Rome— **Monte Cavo**. It is thought that there was once an ancient temple on this spot, and that Hannibal may have camped there, so close, and yet so far, from the city he tried to conquer. As you wind upward, you can see the remains of the old Roman road, a cliff-hanging thriller apparently designed for use by mountain goats. At the top there are winds and the best view anywhere of Rome and the sea and *all* the hill towns at once. And there is a large rambling building which began as a convent, was later transformed into an observatory, and is now a small hotel with a good, though expensive, restaurant.

Only a little further along, in the same southeasterly direction from the city, is **Castel Gandolfo**, a town so ancient that according to legend it was the mother of Rome. It is, of course, known throughout the world today as the traditional summer retreat of the Popes. Once a free duchy, it became the property of the Holy See in the early 17th century, and in 1624 Urban VIII commissioned Carlo Maderna, designer of the façade of St. Peter's, to build the Papal Villa there. Enlarged and enhanced over the centuries, the castle now stands above beautifully terraced Italian gardens, where cypresses and oleanders and rose trees grow in formal rows about the ancient ruins of Domitian's villa.

Papal Gardens at Castel Gandolfo

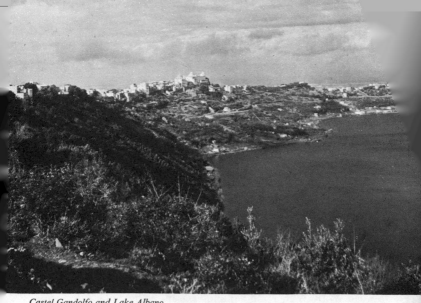

Castel Gandolfo and Lake Albano

In a volcanic crater below the town lies blue **Lake Albano**, much favored in Imperial times by wealthy vacationing Romans. Regattas and mock naval battles were staged there, and many valuable remains of early ships have been found in the clear, deep water. Now a favorite spot for Italian anglers, it is one of the few places you can actually see fish being landed. (There are times, as you watch the indefatigable and luckless fishermen along the banks of the Tiber, that you begin to believe that there *aren't* any fish in Italy.)

PALESTRINA

Palestrina, some twenty miles southeast of Rome by the Via Prenestina, is medieval and thoroughly picturesque, but it is important mainly because of the ruins of the huge *Temple of Fortune.* For years it was known that the temple lay buried there, but lack of funds and the difficulty of excavation made it unlikely that much of it would ever be unearthed. But during World War II, American bombers accidentally accomplished the major part of the job of uncovering the ruins, and archeologists were able to finish the work in 1956. The *Barberini Palace,* which stands over the inner shrine, has been turned into a public museum to house the statues, bronzes, and shards found there. The objects themselves are fascinating, and the museum is splendidly organized to display them. It is said that the director based his plan on that of the Museum of Natural History in New York, a case of the old world learning from the new. The trip to Palestrina is worth while merely to see one mosaic, the largest and most perfect example of that Roman art ever discovered. It has been patiently and perfectly restored and is now magnificently displayed in the museum.

On the road up to Monte Cavo

If you start out for the Alban Hills, then turn southwest (at the intersection with the Via Latina toward the coast, you will be headed toward **Anzio**. The town is now largely rebuilt and restored. The last of the land mines has been found, the barbed wire strands have been removed, and the beach is once again, as it was in the days before the Second World War, a popular and pleasant bathing place. But to get there you must pass by the exact white rows of the British and American military cemeteries, the lasting, tangible evidence of the enormous price of victory. You pass over the high ground held by the German Army and down to the unbelievably tiny foothold of exposed earth the Allied assault forces clung to for more than twelve weeks, until, with the help of forces inching up from Salerno, they were able to break out and force the liberation of Rome. Because it was an open city, Rome shows few marks of the war, but Rome knows that it owes its present existence to those white graves and the scars of war still visible along the way to Anzio.

Next to the modern city of Anzio, and in fact once united with it in one town, is **Nettuno**, the other beach on which the troops came ashore that January night in 1944. Less scarred than Anzio, it is still an excellent example of a medieval walled town with a very well-preserved medieval fortress lowering over it.

Cluster of houses in a hill town near Rome

OSTIA
Directly west of Rome, and connected to it by a stretch of swift superhighway (and by subway as well), lies the old port of the city— Ostia. The site of several important archeological excavations, it is well preserved in spite of the fact that from its earliest days Ostia was subject to repeated attacks by pirates and hostile navies. Among the most important monuments are: the *Temple of Vulcan,* the *baths,* an ancient Roman fire-brigade station, the imperial *Palace of Hadrian,* the temples of *Mithra* and *Cybele,* and the *Palace of the Guilds.* Perhaps the most pleasing ruin is that of a very large Roman theater from the time of the Emperor Agrippa. Here, in a setting of imperial splendor, plays are still occasionally presented.

The beach at Lido di Roma

Bordering Ostia is the **Lido di Roma**, *the* Roman beach. It is crowded and gay, a thoroughly Italian beach with umbrellas and cabañas, bronzed Roman bodies in the briefest of bikinis, and the calm sparkle of the sea. It is so easy to reach that Romans think nothing of taking a couple of hours off in the middle of a hot summer's day and going out for a dip and some sun and sea breeze before the afternoon business hours.

CIVITAVECCHIA

On the coast less than fifty miles northwest of Rome is Civitavecchia. Along the old Via Aurelia, now a modern highway paralleling the railroad, you drive in the shade of tall umbrella pines and
cross quiet fields of grain and pasture land. But this is beach country
too. Almost anywhere along the way you can turn off the Via Aurelia
and in a few minutes be basking on a beach—in an exclusive resort
like **Fregene**, with expensive villas hidden among the pines and the
oleanders, or at a less fashionable spot like **Ladispoli**. Nearer to
Civitavecchia are two especially attractive beaches, each with its own
pleasant prescription for relaxation, which offer pleasant and con-
trasting possibilities for a day or so by the sea. **Santa Marinella** is a
popular resort (though not nearly so much so as Lido di Roma) with
a wide beach, good shops, excellent seafood restaurants, and all the
colorful excitement of Romans on holiday. **Santa Severa**, just to the
south of Santa Marinella, has not yet been "discovered," and so, in
addition to having one of the best beaches along the coast, still retains
much of its old air of restful village simplicity. The beach is shadowed
by a 9th-century Norman castle, whose four towers and keep jut out
into the sea. Within the outer walls of this castle is an almost perfectly
(and accidentally) preserved medieval village, where the people connected with the castle—farmers and fishermen and their families—
still live and work. By simply walking through a gateway in the wall
you enter the Middle Ages. Santa Severa is so unspoiled that the people living in and around the castle haven't had a chance to think of
themselves as curiosities. Only occasional tourists go to the trouble
of wandering in to look around.

If you are looking for a day at the beach in beautifully simple and
uncomplicated surroundings where excellent wine and delicious seafood are plentiful and inexpensive, Santa Severa is your objective—
for a little while yet, at least.

Entrance to Etruscan tomb near Cerveteri

Etruscan sarcophagus in the museum at Tarquinia

All through this country and north of it the ancient Etruscans built their cities and ports. Nearest of these Etruscan centers, midway between Rome and Civitavecchia, is the **Necropolis of Cerveteri**. The city itself is medieval, but near it is a large Etruscan cemetery, a square mile or so of the characteristically domed earth tombs, where you will see examples of the remarkable and highly developed Etruscan art of wall painting. As you see them here in the tombs, you will realize that even the fine collections in Roman museums cannot communicate the same urgent sense of the closeness to us of these vibrant, civilized people who are now such a mystery. It is a strange paradox that they seem to spring to life most vividly in tombs.

A more recently excavated necropolis, and thus one with more untouched objects and better preserved wall paintings, is near **Tarquinia**, some twelve to fifteen miles beyond Civitavecchia. The largest yet to be excavated, it has an enormous variety of Etruscan wall painting, ranging over four hundred years from the 6th to the 2nd century B.C.

UMBRIA

Almost due north of Rome, out along the Via Flaminia, are the hill towns of Umbria. These are real hills, and the Umbrian countryside is quite different from the *campagna* immediately around Rome. The colors are more subtle, the hills are stark and rocky, and the country often looks lonely and harsh. Walled and perched high on craggy peaks, even little towns have a strong fortress quality. None of which makes Umbria sound attractive or beautiful. Actually it is both, and for almost all visitors these medieval hill towns are among the most captivating in Italy. Here it was that 19th-century American travelers found the Europe that they so admired, and writers like Hawthorne discovered a strange and brittle mood which they wove into their stories. Taste has changed greatly since then, but the subtle and indefinable charm of the hill towns has not diminished.

In the past, these handsome hill towns were not considered part of the environs of Rome, but by car or bus it is now possible to get all the way up to Assisi, or even Perugia, and back in one day without undue strain. The American concept of distance and mobility has had its effect in Italy since the war, and the environs of Rome have been greatly extended. A small, but indicative, example of the change is the fact that Gian-Carlo Menotti's "Festival of Two World's," located in the interesting medieval city of **Spoleto,** serves as an important part of the entertainment scene of Rome. Romans who a few years ago would have considered the trip to Spoleto a journey, rather than an excursion, now think nothing of driving up to Spoleto in the evening and returning to the city after the performace. The same is true generally. With an early morning start from Rome you can lunch in Assisi, enjoy an afternoon of sight-seeing, and be back in the city by dinner time.

Similarly, good roads and rapid transportation have brought Rome closer to the south. It is quite possible—though certainly not advisable for sight-seers—to go as far south as Naples and back in a day. What this does mean, however, is that the relatively unspoiled coastline from Terracina to the south is now easily accessible on excursions from Rome. There are few towns along the way and long stretches of pristine beach.

The extension of the environs of Rome is, of course, most meaningful for the traveler who is not unreasonably pressed for time. For the refreshment of body and spirit after the plenitude of Rome, he can now turn to dozens of varied and fascinating experiences that were once far beyond his reach. If you are taking time to savor and study the city, you may well find that your pleasure is increased by an occasional break from the routine of sight-seeing. And it is certain that if you learn to know the surroundings of Rome—the earth from which the city sprang—you will have a finer and deeper appreciation of the city and all that it is and has been.

126